SAY IT NOW! SAY IT RIGHT!

How to Handle Tough or Tender Conversations

MARY J. NESTOR

Say It Now! Say It Right!

First edition published in 2016
Second edition published in 2021 by

Panoma Press Ltd
48 St Vincent Drive, St Albans, Herts, AL1 5SJ, UK
info@panomapress.com
www.panomapress.com

Book layout by Neil Coe.

978-1-784529-42-0

Dedication

This book is dedicated to my sisters – Ethel, Barbara, Frances, and Veronica – the strongest, most fearless, resourceful, funny, and "SAY IT NOW! SAY IT RIGHT!" women I know and whom I deeply love and admire. They are wonderful role models for their baby sister, more than they will ever know.

Acknowledgements

So many people have helped me along the way to Say it Now! and Say it Right! and I owe them a big Thank You. This book is dedicated to my earliest manager and mentor, Dave Lotoki, who once told me I had the talent to "piss people off." Who knew that "talent" would later become the basis for this book? To Charlene Rothkopf, then the Director of Benefits at Marriott Corporate, who sat me down more than once to let me know I wasn't exactly Saying it Right in my role as a new supervisor at Marriott Corporation. To the Dale Carnegie Organization, which showed me how to Say it Now! and Say it Right! and overcome my crippling fear of public speaking and win the highest award for achievement pen at the end of the 12-week Basic Course (I think Session 5 was a breakthrough moment).

To great mentors and fellow Toastmasters in Savannah Toastmasters Club 705, who trusted me as their President and taught me so many lessons on how to Say it Now! and Say it Right! in a leadership role, especially Grant Washington, who was a kind but merciless evaluator and always found something for me to improve on. And to Dave Newman, who "kicked my butt" in a live webinar training session when I was ready to lose focus and give up on rebranding and relaunching my speaking, coaching, and consulting business under Say it Now! and Say it Right! They were the models for Say it Now! and Say it Right! (although the jury is still out on Dave's butt kicking in the Say it Right! category).

Thank you all for caring enough to say what needed to be said at the right time and in a way so that I heard the message and, as you can see from this introduction, never forgot it.

Contents

Section III

Section IV

Section V

Foreword

SAY IT NOW! SAY IT RIGHT! may be the most valuable book you ever read. Pause and consider what I just said, "the most valuable." Many of the world's biggest problems have come from people not speaking up when they should have, or from them speaking out in the wrong way and increasing the problems. Wars have been started or ended by the improper vs proper use of these techniques. The impact of learning the skills and techniques taught in this book can remove many unnecessary obstacles in your life and business and could seriously "rock your world."

Scroll through the table of contents and you will immediately recall situations where you or others could have used these excellent skills.

The courage to communicate and the skill to communicate clearly and appropriately can catapult you past any competitors in circumstances involving human relations.

In some cases, "saying it right" can make the difference between life and death.

In March of 1953 William J. Coughlin wrote an article in Harper's Magazine titled: The Great Mokusatsu Mistake - Was this the deadliest error of our time?

http://alsos.wlu.edu/information.aspx?id=1699

The following description is from ALSOS Digital Library for Nuclear Issues: This article examines the serious consequences of an error in the translation of a response issued by the Cabinet of Japan to the Allies' Potsdam Declaration, a surrender ultimatum, during World War II. Issued by Japanese Premier Kantaro Suzuki, the statement announced that the Cabinet had taken a stance of mokusatsu, *which can be translated as either "making no comment on" or "ignoring" something. According to the article, when the statement was issued, Japan's media construed the message to mean that the Cabinet was ignoring the ultimatum, while the intended message was that comment was being withheld pending an announcement. The article investigates Japan's rebuffed attempts to get the Soviet Union to mediate a peace, the internal debate within the Japanese government over surrender, and the intent of the Cabinet's message. The author asserts that Suzuki's ambiguous choice of wording led directly to the United States government's subsequent use of the atomic bomb against Japan.*

That horrifying example was one that involved translation from one language and culture to another. But isn't that the same when your friend or mate speaks in emotional language and you reply in logical language? Aren't cultures involved when one family or company assumes that its internal rules and practices are also embraced by the other group?

Every day we encounter cultural and language differences, many of which we aren't even aware of, and yet we move blindly ahead as if we already knew enough to be successful with them. More than anything this book will give you the courage to speak up when you should, the wisdom to know when to remain quiet, and the skills to speak well when you do. You will learn to get through to people in the ways that will have the right effect.

Now, let me get out of your way so that you can begin the discovery of these powerful ideas.

In the Spirit of Growth,

Jim Cathcart, CSP, CPAE
Past President of the National Speakers Association
And author of Relationship Selling
Founder of Cathcart.com

SECTION I

SAY IT NOW!

CHAPTER 1

Finding My Voice

I grew up in a big family in Gary, Indiana. Between the eight of us – two parents, five girls and one boy – we probably had a total of 10 significant conversations between all of us. Oh, there were lively discussions at the Sunday dinner table about that morning's Sunday sermon, but aside from that, there wasn't a whole lot of conversation going on among us. Even among siblings. It was almost as if we weren't supposed to say things to each other, or about each other, or about what was going on in our lives…our thoughts, dreams, and aspirations. Or what was going on at all. As the youngest, I was probably the

> "Keep it to yourself," could have been the family motto.

most silent, and the most observant. There was a lot I wanted to say, but I learned at an early age that expressing your opinion or observations wasn't something that was acceptable or appreciated. "Keep it to yourself," could have been the family motto.

Not one to always follow the rules, I occasionally ignored the motto. I can remember my mother saying to me, shaking her head, "I never know what's going to come out of your mouth!" In other words, she was telling me to keep quiet. Keep your opinions to yourself. Don't rock the boat. Don't be outspoken. What you have to say isn't necessary or important. Nobody wants to hear from you. So, it wasn't long before I got the message that keeping quiet…and your opinions to yourself…was what was valued and appreciated. If you ventured out, and dared to speak up, you were ridiculed, scolded, and regarded with disdain. Clear message. Understood.

As I got older, I learned my lesson well, but was still observant of the world around me. There were many, many times when I wanted to express my joy, happiness, fear, sorrow, anger, or whatever the emotion, but always held back to fall in line with the unwritten "family rules."

Except for one time. I don't remember how old I was, but I had a very good friend, Julie, whose family lived a couple houses away from my oldest married sister, Ethel. Julie came from a big family, and they were a lot like ours. Not a lot of conversation, but there was a lot of yelling. Julie's father was a drinker, like my father was, but when Julie 's father drank, he got angry.

Little things would set him off, like the dirty dishes in the sink or dust on the furniture. Even though their house was just another tract house, the same as the others on the block, and the furniture was old and mismatched, Julie's dad would complain that it didn't shine and glow like the biggest mansions on Morningside Drive. It was such a day when Julie was about to become the object of her father's wrath, and I was about to find my voice.

I was visiting my sister, who was 13 years older than me, married, with children of her own. I decided to see if Julie could hang out with me for a while. Julie was home but had chores to do. When I came in, she was polishing the furniture with liquid polish and an old cloth. I could hear loud talking from the kitchen, and from Julie's sad look, I knew that something was wrong. She whispered that she had to polish all the furniture before she could play, and that her dad was in one of his "moods," so she had to do a good job. I offered to help her so she could finish faster, so she got me a cloth, and we started polishing with exuberance.

The scratched, worn furniture was past its former glow, but we did our best. After a while, Julie's father came into the room and looked at our work. He raged! "This is sloppy work! The polish is streaked on this table! You're wasting polish and time!" Julie was terrified, and I looked at him with amazement. No one in my family spoke out in this way, whether it was good or bad. I was shocked and scared for Julie. He looked at Julie and said to her, "Go to your room." Julie obediently started for the stairs, with her father right behind. It took just a minute for me to understand that Julie was in serious trouble and something bad was about to happen.

As they slowly began to climb the stairs, something came over me. I walked over to the stairs, looked her father in the eyes, and said, "If you're going to do anything to Julie, you'd better do it to me, too, because I was polishing the furniture, too." I don't know who was more shocked! Me, for speaking out to another adult in such a bold way; Julie, who stopped in mid-climb on the stair and looked at me and her dad and then back to me, open mouth, wild-eyed, waiting without breathing; or Julie's dad, who was being challenged by some sassy little kid.

The rest of the scenario is jumbled. Julie didn't undergo some dreadful punishment that day. I, on the other hand, got a serious talking to from my mother for speaking to an adult this way (my mother having heard the story from Julie's dad via my sister Ethel). Julie and I cemented our friendship with my act of bravery. I felt a little like a hero. I found my voice and risked unknown consequences to defend my friend and save her from whatever punishment awaited her. It was scary and risky, but I knew at that moment I had to say something. If I waited, or if I kept silent, I was sure something terrible would have happened. I didn't know what the outcome of my action would be. Would Julie's father make good on his threat of punishment anyway? Would he punish me too, as I had suggested? Would I get my own from my father when I got home for being rude to an adult? Would Julie's dad see the error of his ways, stop bullying everyone in his family, stop drinking, and become a model father? I had no assumptions or outcomes in my mind. I just knew that I had to Say something Now!

I would like to say that day I got my voice and continued to speak out. A strong talking to and my mother's embarrassment at my hand was enough to renew the family motto. There were times that I spoke out, but not with the grand results of that scene at Julie's house.

> I just knew that I had to say something NOW!

There are many opportunities that come and go without saying what needs to be said. It's not just personal situations, like this story, but business, workplace, leadership, management, organizational, and community situations where someone with the courage to take a risk and make a statement, express an idea or opposing viewpoint, can make a difference.

What moments in time stand out where you were able to say what needed to be said? On the opposite side of that question, what conversations are you avoiding? How has a "code of silence" or family rules or just the expectation to always be "nice" and positive affected your ability to have the tough (or tender) conversations in your personal or work life? Do office politics, an unethical manager, or dictatorial leaders create a culture of silence and expected agreement? Do employees keep important ideas or information to themselves rather than risk retribution and rebuke? Do you put up with a less than satisfying relationship or life situation because you don't want to speak up and "rock the boat?"

What conversation, statement or answer do you regret not having that could have changed the course of your life or someone you cared about? What did you need to Say it Now! but didn't? What do you need to Say it Now! but don't know how to Say it Right!?

The purpose of this book is to help you recognize the moments when you have an opportunity – maybe a once-in-a-lifetime chance to say what needs to be said and avoid making these mistakes. You will learn how to speak up at the right time – when to Say it Now! – and in the right way – how to Say it Right! Both of these elements have to be in place for you to achieve what you want your intervention to achieve. Saying something at the right time but in a destructive manner is useless. Saying something perfectly right but way past the time it can be effective is equally useless. In the first section of this book, you will learn how to Say it Now! In the second section, you will learn how to Say it Right! In the third section, I will offer different scenarios and show you how to Say it Now! and Say it Right! for each situation.

What did you need to SAY IT NOW! But didn't?

The lack of authentic, honest, direct, and timely conversations is robbing people of love, enjoyment, work satisfaction, and authentic, healthy relationships. It prevents businesses from tapping the creativity, talents, ideas, and solutions from all levels of employees. The reluctance, or inability, for employees to Say it Now! and Say it Right! is responsible for bad decisions that lead to small problems and major disasters.

Many years after the incident with Julie's dad, my first marriage came to an end. At that time, one of my sisters said to me, "We (my four sisters) wondered why you wanted to marry him (my first husband). We knew it wasn't a good match. We didn't think you should have married him and tried to tell you." She meant it in a caring, loving way, but my thought was, after all this time, why are you telling me now? I was astonished and sad. When I asked my sister why they didn't confront me before the wedding, she said they figured I wouldn't have listened to them.

There were lots of reasons why I shouldn't have gotten married when I did, and not because of the person I was marrying. Out of five girls in the family, I was the youngest. Though my older sisters excelled in academics and some even got scholarship offers, the expectation for the girls in my family was to graduate from high school, get a job, and get married (in that order).

My only brother was born after sister #4, and he not only was expected to go to college, but he also excelled beyond expectations and eventually graduated from Notre Dame. By the time I graduated high school, either times had changed or my parents were more easily persuaded. After waiting two years after my own high school graduation for my brother to graduate college, I was allowed to go away to Marquette University. I had a chance at an education that could have launched my career in journalism and an exciting life writing, traveling, and meeting interesting people all over the world.

When my father became ill my second year at Marquette University and my parents could no longer pay for the private college I was attending, I panicked. I just couldn't face going back home to the silence and the broken place my home had become;

no longer a child but expected to live as one in my parents' home again. When I got the chance, through a complicated set of circumstances, I made my escape and accepted a marriage proposal from someone I barely knew. He was someone I admired, I liked, and was considered by my mother as "acceptable" husband material. He had a good job in romantic San Francisco, California, which meant this marriage had the added bonus of moving across the country, far away from life as I knew it.

My sisters were surprised I was getting married to an almost complete stranger and questioned what I was doing. If they had sat me down and had an intervention of sorts, and told me all the reasons I was going to make the biggest mistake of my life, would I have listened? Would my sisters have been right? No one will ever know. Would I have been shocked but honored and felt valued if they had been honest and persistent about their reservations? Would I have known that they cared? Would I have felt loved? Yes! Would I have changed my mind? Not even I know the answer to that question. But when I am asked this question – *If you could change one decision you made in the course of your life, what would that be?* – my answer is to stay in school at Marquette University and not run off and escape my life at my parents' home by getting married.

One final comment. This is not a book that will teach you to finally get even with people who've "done you wrong." It's not a green light to blast those you don't like or become everyone's critic. It is a book on finding your voice – on learning how and when to have those conversations, whether tough or tender, at the right moment, and in the right way – from a place of caring and selflessness – so that you're heard by the other person. It's about recognizing when you need to speak up and how to convey your message in the right way for every situation.

I've learned a lot of lessons about communication since that occasion with Julie and her father. I've made mistakes. I've also had some wonderful teachers and mentors along the way who had the courage, love, and concern to Say it Now! when I needed to hear something. There were times when I was about to go over the cliff – again – and their honest, tough (and sometimes tender) words brought me back from a crippling fall. I've learned to Say it Now! and Say it Right! from these generous people. The conversations weren't always easy or comfortable. It's amazing how later in life those people who intervened with a strong rebuke remember my strengths and value our relationships. I've learned to shake off the warnings of my childhood and Say it Now! and Say it Right! My desire for you, after reading this book and working through the exercises, is that you will, too.

CHAPTER 2

Be Nice?

"If you can't say something nice, don't say anything at all."
Every mother on the planet to her child

How many times have you heard that phrase? If you can't say something nice, or positive, or complimentary, don't open your mouth. Being nice was equated with saying something nice, regardless of the situation, your feelings, observations, or the impending doom about to happen. Being nice was always being complimentary. Being agreeable. Being part of the "team." Anything that even hinted at the negative, or a possible problem or situation was to be avoided.

OK. It's nice to be nice. It's nice to compliment someone. To give them positive feedback. To affirm their decisions, ideas, or conclusions. But is being nice always the best course of action in every situation? What is being nice anyway?

Early in my career at Marriott, I was a new supervisor in the Benefits Administration Department of their Corporate Headquarters in Bethesda, Maryland. I was so green; I didn't have any management or supervisory training. I did have a good reputation as an executive assistant who took my responsibilities seriously, and that's what prompted a former manager to recruit me to an open supervisory position in her department.

As a new supervisor, I had an opportunity to give a presentation to a group of senior managers. I don't even remember the topic. I was nervous and yet excited about the opportunity to have such great exposure to the top managers in my department.

The presentation was after lunch, and I met with one of my team members to go over the PowerPoint and handouts before the presentation. Everything was set, and I gave the presentation with confidence and lots of energy. I could see that things were going well, since everyone seemed to be enjoying the presentation. They were all smiling at me and nodding in agreement.

After the presentation, I slipped into the ladies' room to freshen up. While I was washing my hands, I looked closely in the mirror, and to my horror, I noticed that I had a very noticeable piece of broccoli in my front tooth! No wonder the managers were smiling at me. I was horrified and humiliated! There I was thinking that their smiles indicated they liked the presentation when they were really trying not to laugh at the broccoli caught between my teeth.

Mortified, I ran back to my office and encountered the staff member who helped me prep before the presentation. "Joanne," I said. "I can't believe I just gave that whole presentation in front of those managers with a piece of broccoli in my teeth." She looked at me sheepishly, and whispered, "I know." "What! You know! I mean, you knew I had broccoli stuck in my teeth and didn't say anything?" "I'm sorry," said Joanne. "I saw it but didn't want to embarrass you by saying something."

I couldn't believe it! Here I was, going to make the presentation of my life (at least at that point in my career it was the biggest opportunity) and someone who knew I was in a position to make a fool of myself didn't warn me and save me from embarrassment?

Joanne thought she was being "nice" not to tell me something that was embarrassing. Actually, it was embarrassing for her to point out anything that she thought wasn't positive to her boss. To her, telling me about this would be saying something negative, and she was taught to always be positive. She was saving herself the embarrassment of having to tell her boss something uncomplimentary. But what about me?

What is being nice? Was it nice to say nothing and hope somehow that the broccoli would fall out of my tooth in time so I wouldn't be embarrassed in front of the group? Was it nice to keep silent when a comment, no matter who was embarrassed, could have saved another person from a bad situation? I've always said that nice people aren't always the ones who always have something positive to say. Often the nicest person shows they care about you by pointing out the "broccoli in your teeth," which could be any number of things. Your bra strap is showing. Your fly is unzipped. You've got toilet paper stuck to your shoe. You left the price tag on your new shirt. Your skirt is too tight, and your underwear is showing through. Is it "nice" to always say everything is fine when something is terribly wrong?

I think "nice" takes on a whole new meaning in the context of Say it Now! and Say it Right! My assistant could have taken the bold step by saying something like, "This is awkward for me to mention this, but you have some broccoli wedged in your upper front tooth." The time

> Often the nicest person shows they care about you by pointing out the "broccoli in your teeth."

to tell me that was before I gave the presentation, not afterwards. Say it Now! has everything to do with timing. What makes it difficult is the timing isn't always comfortable or enough in advance of the situation at hand to Say it Right!

Honest criticism has taken a bad rap. We don't even call it criticism anymore. Too harsh. Too, well, critical.

"Constructive feedback" is a nicer phrase. "Positive feedback" is also another way to put it. I'm all for using whatever words make it easier to Say it Now! to intervene or to help someone become better, stronger, more effective, productive, and confident. If you want to call it being nice, great.

Unfortunately, the education system, the change in parenting philosophies, everyone being on a "team" or everyone expecting and getting a ribbon or prize just for participating has diluted or eliminated the transformative power of honest – and at times not-so-nice – direct feedback. If your Aunt Vivian always puts too much salt in the soup for the weekly family dinners, and everyone hates the soup, and everyone knows it but her, is that being nice? Nice to sit there sipping the salty soup, knowing that by letting her know nicely that the soup is too salty, the soup would be so much better and everyone would avoid salt bloat the next day?

Or what about your child who isn't athletic, doesn't like competition, and gets a stomachache every time he has to go to T-ball practice? Do you tell him he's doing great, high-five as he comes off the field, week after week, dejected and in tears? Yes! Helping people through difficult learning experiences is more than nice. It's character building. It's showing support, love. He may feel he isn't good at T-ball. Yet, you are trying to be nice and encouraging.

Sometimes children, or even adults, know their shortcomings and would like a way out of a losing situation, but feel that someone in authority (a parent or manager) needs to let them off the hook. In those situations, being nice means being honest. Being nice may be taking the risk to help people deal with reality. It's allowing people to make their own choices, even at a young age. It's being supportive of decisions, even if it's not your choice or is against your wishes.

Being "nice" can be a way of ducking responsibility or avoiding situations that need attention. Like saying nothing to a friend who wears clothing too tight (too old, too dirty, too wrinkled, too inappropriate) to the point that it's affecting his or her job, credibility, professional image, etc. Or avoiding telling colleagues or employees that people don't want to talk to them because they come across as unfriendly, unapproachable, or just plain hard to deal with. That's a difficult conversation to have. But if you're the boss, and you get complaints over a period of time, who is responsible for a recurring problem? If they had confronted the issue at the first complaint and coached the employee on how to effectively deal with others, the rest of the complaints may have never happened. So, is the employee really at fault for continuing behavior that he was unaware of, but of which the boss was informed?

> Being nice may be taking the risk to help people deal with reality.

You may be nice to yourself by avoiding uncomfortable situations, but you are not being nice to the offending individual. Say your friend has an annoying habit. Or a friend uses inappropriate language. Or a co-worker (or boss) stands a little too close when he talks to others or makes inappropriate personal comments about appearance. Is it nice to let this person continue? It may be more comfortable to just ignore it, or laugh it off, but things aren't going to change. If you notice it, others will too. And if it continues, chances are no one else is going to confront the person. Be "nice" to everyone and Say it Now! to this individual.

I like to enter 5Ks around Savannah. I'm not a runner by any stretch of the word. I recently ran the Rock 'N Roll 5K in Savannah, Georgia. It was held on a Sunday, after the main half- and full marathon on Saturday. It was a dreary, cold, and rainy day at Daffin Park, but the crowd was large and on fire. We dodged rain puddles and made it through to the end. As I came across the finish line, far behind the front runners, I felt great. I jogged (well, my version) all the way, which was a first for me. I ran under the inflatable arch at the finish line with the Rock 'n' Roll Marathon logo, just like the front runners with my arms overhead in victory, knowing that the cameras were snapping my picture for a photo finish. On the other side, I received a medal that said "5K finisher." That was nice. I showed up and made it to the finish line, and I am proud of that medal. There is great satisfaction in doing a good job, winning a race, making your best contribution. Even in just participating in an event. No one can say that I didn't deserve it.

When you get a medal, or a raise, or a promotion, or recognition that is not deserved or earned, it rings hollow. You know it, and everyone else does, too. Getting an "exceeds expectations" on an annual review is "nice," but if there are things you need to improve on, isn't it better to take the feedback and know that, after some work on your part, you earned that raise, promotion, or medal at the end of the race?

Nice is telling your three-year-old that the crayon lines, squiggles, and dots really are a beautiful picture of a dog, or tree, or the family. Telling a co-worker that his PowerPoint presentations are great, when in fact they are too wordy, dull, or out of sequence, isn't nice. It's a disservice to him and the poor people who have to suffer through them. It lets the person do less than his best. Sometimes the best way to be nice is to just Say it Now! before it's too late. Saying it Now! can turn out to be the nicest thing you can do.

CHAPTER 3

Before You SAY IT AT ALL! Check Your Motive

Emily was a bright new staff member. Eager, energetic, passionate about her job and the customers. She had a tireless work ethic, contributed new ideas in staff meetings, and had excellent organizational skills. Despite her age and limited work experience, she caught the eye of senior management early on. She was a go-getter and had potential. That put her on the company's fast-track list. Unfortunately, for some staff members, she was perceived as a threat. In contrast, they came off as lazy, content, and unimaginative.

Following company protocol, Emily shared a new idea for reorganizing the work reporting calendar that would save time and money with Bob, Emily's team leader. Now Bob, who had recently been passed over for promotion for not being innovative, was a little jealous of the attention Emily was getting. He praised her new idea and encouraged her to bring it up in the next team meeting.

After getting Bob's endorsement, she confidently announced it in the next staff meeting. To her shock, Bob immediately began to point out all the flaws, adding that Emily's immaturity and lack of understanding of "how things work around here" was the cause of her bad idea. Emily was embarrassed and felt betrayed. Bob's peers gave him the nod for taking the opportunity to bring her down a notch or two.

Did Emily really have a bad idea? Maybe. Did she deserve to be embarrassed by her manager in front of a group? Never. Bob may have enjoyed his moment, but the time to tell her about the idea's flaws was in the first private meeting. Check your motives. To Bob, it wasn't about the idea's merits. It was an opportunity to Say it Now! for all the wrong reasons.

What was gained (a moment of public embarrassment for a co-worker) is nothing in comparison to what was lost for so many:

- Emily doesn't trust her team leader; she's angry and resentful.

- Emily doesn't trust herself as much.

- Emily isn't going to offer her ideas to her team leader or the team in a public setting (great ideas lost).

- Bob, though he thinks he won, really lost – Emily's support, the rest of the team's trust (will he do this to me?), and probably senior managers in the meeting who know about his being passed over for promotion.

- Bob comes off looking unsupportive and unprofessional.

- Senior management may not give Emily as much support or credit as she deserves.

- The idea may have been great or at least worth discussing, saving the company time and money.

- Bob's future comments may come into question, after showing he can be negative and cruel.

As I mentioned before, the Say it Now! is not a green light to tell everyone off, point out everyone's faults and failings, embarrass people, or become the powerful OZ in your Emerald City. Say it Now! should be used sparingly, as one tool in the leadership toolbox. It comes from a place of building up, not tearing down. It is used for disaster prevention. Honestly examine your motives. Don't try to fool yourself. Don't Say it Now! if any of these are true:

> It comes from a place of building up, not tearing down.

- **You don't like a person and want to "take them down a notch" in a public setting.** There is a dark side to everyone, no matter how "nice" they are. You can say the nicest thing with the wrong motives. Maybe you see that person as a competitor. They're just a little smarter, quicker, or more well-liked than you are. So, you take the opportunity to shoot down an idea in a meeting. "No, that won't work." "We tried that last year and it was a disaster." "Come on, are you serious? That's the worst idea yet." All those statements may be true, but really, do you have to say them at the morning staff meeting in front of everyone? No!

- **You want to cause friction or promote your own personal agenda.** I had a manager once who enjoyed setting people up just to see how they would handle it. He would assign two managers to oversee the same project without informing the other, and then sit back and see how they handled the confusion. No, this wasn't professional development or leadership training. It was more for his own personal entertainment. Yes, though infrequent, there are people out there like that.

- **You have some information that could cause two people to end a relationship.** Are you feeling miserable or lonely or hurt? Suffering from your own breakup or betrayal? Just can't stand that two people who love each other have problems (doesn't everyone) and are trying to work things out? You just happen to know (from reliable sources) that Jerome is cheating on Sally. Isn't it your duty to tell Sally what's going on? Not if you just want someone else to join your pity party in the Realm of the Miserable Rejects! This kind of intervention can be the right thing to do with the right motive and right time.

- **You're angry (at the person, at the situation, just feeling angry today).** Never have one of these Say it Now! conversations when you're angry and just feel like venting. Stop. Think. Cool off. Check your motive (don't be Bob) and proceed if you've got your head and heart straight. This goes for texting, emailing, and posting on social media as well.

> Never have one of these SAY IT NOW! conversations when you're angry and just feel like venting. Stop. Think. Cool off.

- **You are jealous of a friendship between two co-workers and feel left out,** so you start playing one against the other in hopes of becoming someone's best friend.

I remember the lyrics from the Beatles song, "...Ah, look at all the lonely people." There are lots of them, who for one reason or another have created their own loneliness and start looking for friendship or approval or love at work, volunteer groups, book clubs, or at yoga class. Lonely, unhappy people want someone to notice and care about them. What they can't handle is when everyone else seems to be happy and accepted and loved. "Why can't that be me?" They don't see themselves as putting off negative vibes strong enough to bring down a concrete and steel skyscraper faster than a 9.5 California earthquake.

- **You want to promote yourself to the boss** by inflating an incident with another co-worker in hopes it will put that co-worker in a bad light and make yours shine a little brighter. Attempts at manipulation never work out. Sooner or later the spotlight turns on you, revealing just where the deceit lies. And, the next time you make a mistake, everyone is happy to point the finger of accusation at you. Delighted, even.

- **You waited too long.** Coming in after the fact just exposes your inability to act boldly and decisively. It's just an "I told you so" that doesn't help anyone. Some people who are too cowardly to Say it Now! at the appropriate time try to redeem themselves by putting another sword into the body. Coming in late begs the question: why didn't you say something? This creates a different kind of distrust and encourages justifiable paranoia with team members who wonder what mistakes they are making that they don't know about now but will be revealed at a later time.

> Coming in after the fact just exposes your inability to act boldly and decisively.

- **You want to criticize someone without helping them change and improve.** Managers do this when they don't address employee performance issues and pile on the criticism in an annual performance review. The time to address issues is as they happen, not as a "gotcha" at the end of the year. I was told early on in my career in Human Resources that a manager's job was to support, train, and coach employees. The manager's job and HR were to help people succeed, not keep score of an employee's failings and mistakes. Losing a job, missing a promotion or opportunity, can be devastating. Before going through with a termination of employment, I was told to ask the question, "Have we (as a company, manager, HR) done everything possible to help this person succeed?" If the answer is "no," then put on the brakes, give the person another chance, find out what help hasn't yet been offered, and try again.

> The time to address issues is as they happen, not as a "Gotcha" at the end of the year.

- **You start your comments with, "You're Wrong!"** No one wants to hear this. In whose opinion? Who said so? Why? Unless they just said that 2 + 2 = 5, there is room for interpretation in almost anything. If you want a fight on your hands, just tell someone they are wrong. After some discussion, you (and the other person) may agree that they were wrong. But "You're wrong!" isn't the best opening statement.

> Unless they just said that 2 + 2 = 5, there is room for interpretation in almost anything.

The purpose of speaking out at the right time (say it now) with the right message is awareness and possible change. What if you get the timing wrong? Any of the following reactions are possible.

- **The other person gets angry and starts to tell you off (in public?).** Not a pleasant situation. It could be their volatile personality, or they've had a bad day and your comment, though well-intended, is the last straw. Public places are rarely the best platform for a tough conversation.

- **Broken relationships.** Whether business or professional, stepping out to Say it Now! has a risk. Despite your best intentions, the other person may feel attacked and embarrassed. If your relationship is on shaky legs to begin with, your comment may be confirmation that you're a friend not worth having.

- **An embarrassing moment for everyone.** Now, you would expect that. In fact, one tip is to begin by saying something like, "This is a little awkward and even embarrassing for me, and may be for you, but I have something to share with you that may be to your benefit." Wait for a response. If they say, "Go ahead," then you've got permission. If they say, "I've had a terrible day and can't take any more feedback," save it for later. Respect a person's wishes, keep the friendship, but be on the lookout for another opportunity to share your message.

- **They don't get it and think you're just being critical.** If you don't get the Say it Right! part right, you may come off as critical and blaming. It's not just your words, but tone of voice and body language. If your intention is to build up, your words have to match your body language.

- **Their feelings are hurt**. Begin with, "I don't want to hurt your feelings by bringing this up, and my intention is to help. If I'm off base, please tell me and the conversation is over." That gives your friend control of the situation and not feeling like they are being put upon.

- **You come off as "holier than thou" and judgmental.** Starting a conversation with the word "You" can sound blaming and accusatory. "You are a jerk." "You shouldn't have said that to Joe in the meeting." "You're always taking a negative approach and everyone is sick of it. Watch how I respond to things in meetings. I never come across as negative." Oh, yeah? Well, how about now? Who's the jerk? Holding yourself up as the gold standard is risky since no one is perfect.

- **People clam up around you,** since they feel that you're looking for a reason to be critical. If you're a manager or supervisor or team leader, this is the worst possible situation. You'd rather people tell you off or complain to your face than talk behind your back or withhold valuable information that can help (or hurt) the organization. When your team members come to you with information or questions or complaints, reserve judgment and reaction. Say something like, "I can see you feel strongly about this. What's going on? What's happening?" And then stop talking and keep listening. The more people share, the better you'll understand what's really going on. The first iteration is usually not the whole story.

- **You could be labeled as not being positive or "nice."** The nicest thing you can do is to learn to speak up, for your sake and the sake of the person you care about. They won't always get it.

> The more people share, the better you'll understand what's really going on.

- **They get mad and think you're a jerk.** OK, maybe it takes being a jerk at times to convey an important message. You can't control what other people think of you. The best thing I ever heard, which is all over the internet and attributed to lots of sources is, "What other people think of you is none of your business." You can control your message (the words you use), the timing/setting, and your motive. The rest is up for grabs.

- **They don't listen and keep it up.** What a person does with information is up to them. Message conveyed. Depending on the situation (someone drinking and about to drive, constantly skipping school, stealing from the company), you may need reinforcements. Even then, know when your intervention is ineffective and move on.

- **They don't listen and ramp it up – they get worse just to make you angry.** Be careful. A little pushback is expected. Is this person likely to do some harm, or God forbid, come back with a gun (it happens when least expected)? Be careful and get help (your boss, a counselor, the police) if necessary.

> You can control your message (the words you use), the timing/setting, and your motive. The rest is up for grabs.

- **They retaliate by trying to discredit you.** Not knowing the formula for Say it Now! Say it Right! they say it wrong and at the wrong time and place. Ouch! This depends on how you are perceived, the other person's level of professionalism, and how you handled the first Say it Now! opportunity.

When your motives are right, and the timing is right, taking the risk to Say it Now! can be transformational. On the plus side, they may:

- **Thank you.** Your boss may not know she used the word "like" or "OK" like salt on movie theater popcorn every time she gave a presentation or just spoke up in a meeting. Your spouse may not realize that he has a nasty habit of questioning you (about everything) in public. A co-worker may not realize her emails are full of grammatical mistakes, making her messages look unprofessional and sloppy.

- **They improve**. Awareness puts them on a path to change. Hooray!

- **Relationships get stronger**. It may be difficult to hear about your personal "broccoli in the teeth," but what a relief to be able to get rid of a nasty habit that is evident to everyone but you! **This** is being nice and caring. **This** is a real friend, for someone to take a risk to speak out for your benefit.

- **Open new dialogues.** When you realize that your boss or co-worker has the courage to finally confront you with the intention of coaching to higher performance, you've found a friend you can confide in. Are there others that need attention? You may have co-workers or staff that you need to talk to as well. Can this person be a mentor to show you how to effectively Say it Now! and Say it Right!? A culture of accepting feedback encourages dialogue, giving people permission to open up and share ideas and information.

- **New self-awareness.** Sometimes it takes several Say it Now! moments in a person's life for them to finally get it. If uncomfortable or negative situations keep recurring at points in your life, you may be at a loss, since no one has ever had the courage or caring to bring it up in a positive and honest way. Many people are wandering through life, stumbling over the same roadblocks, and not knowing why. It's hard to see our own reflection in the mirror the way others do.

  You can control your message (the words you use), the timing/setting, and your motive. The rest is up for grabs.

CHAPTER 4

Say It Later... And Count The Cost

When my daughter was in college in the Midwest, we were living in Rockville, Maryland. That summer, she got a job and moved to Ocean City, Maryland, with some of her friends from high school. As fate would have it, she met a young man she felt was the love of her life. On her return from Ocean City at the end of summer, she announced that she didn't want to return to her college but was "in love" and was set on following her new boyfriend to San Francisco, where she would get a job and go to school, while he did the same. After much discussion (lots of Say it Now! moments), she left for San Francisco and the beginning of what she thought would be an exciting adventure.

The glamorous life they imagined turned out to be a constant grind of working and going to school, with little time or money for anything else. It didn't take long before the real life of school, work, and conflicting schedules took the glow off the adventure. By Thanksgiving, she decided that life was too hard and wanted to come home. Of course, I was delighted, and after making some arrangements, I flew out to San Francisco a few days before Christmas to "rescue" my daughter.

After packing her Chevy Geo with all her possessions, we headed south to Bakersfield and then across country, trying to beat the winter storms in the mountains. We hit a pothole somewhere outside of Albuquerque, New Mexico, and didn't know we just about shredded one of the back tires. At 80 miles an hour, the tire held together, but the 18-wheeler that pulled up beside us could see we were moments away from disaster. Two women alone in the middle of nowhere, I wasn't about to pull over and kept going until the next exit. Only then did we hear the "klump, klump" of our shredded tire and realized the trucker was trying to save our lives. There isn't always a chance to say something later. Say it Now!

There's no reason to wait to tell someone a fault or shortcoming that is visible to everyone but is one they may not be aware of. I didn't know I had broccoli in my teeth when I gave my presentation. I couldn't see my teeth unless I looked in a mirror. But every time I smiled or talked, there it was, for all to see. I could see the trucker, frantically waving and honking his horn, but not the tire that could have flown off at any moment, sending us careening off the road or into

> There isn't always a chance to say something later. SAY IT NOW!

oncoming traffic. Say it Now! before one more embarrassing or tragic moment goes by.

The Cost of NOT SAYING IT AT ALL:

- **Disasters.** Think of a friend that had a disastrous relationship, bought a house that was a money pit, or had an accident after drinking and driving. There is no pleasure saying, "I told you so." It may cost you money to pay for a cab, or hours spent with a friend who is getting over a breakup, but the cost is small compared to having to visit that friend in the hospital, a victim (again?) at the hands of a brutal partner, or taking someone in after they lost their home to foreclosure.

- **Continued bad habits**. Habits become invisible to the person who has them. Even the most disgusting habits, like picking your nose, or cleaning your teeth with the end of a cocktail straw, or sucking your teeth, or wiping your runny nose with your sleeve (add your own). Please, say it now – gently, lovingly – but hold up the mirror for the clueless individual who is grossing out the rest of us unaware.

- **Errors.** If you don't speak up, errors can become disasters. In this case, say it the first time it happens. I worked with a manager who had an employee who made mistakes that cost time and money and even forced the manager to correct them herself. She was a very "nice" person who kept saying, "No one is perfect," which is true, while taking her time to fix this employee's mistakes. If an employee needs training to correct errors, make it available. If the system is causing the errors, get a new one. If you, as the manager, keep fixing other people's mistakes, you're just enabling them to continue to do substandard work and not have to take responsibility for their work quality. If all else fails and mistakes continue, they either don't care (why should they, you're going to take care of it) or they just don't have the ability and should move on to a place where they can be successful.

- **Lost revenue/business.** Sometimes you have to ask for the business or a raise or your highest fee. If you don't Say it Now! money left on the table is lost forever.

- **Lost relationships.** Are you always negative? Are you good at the Say it Now! but everything that comes out of your mouth is a criticism? Say it Now! is also saying the positive, loving, helpful things that others need to hear. Don't hold back. Say it Now! I love you! I need you! I want you! I forgive you! I care about you! You're important to me! You're doing a great job! The right moment passes quickly. Sometimes saying the kind, loving, positive things are the scariest, hardest of all.

> SAY IT NOW! is also saying the positive, loving, helpful things that others need to hear.

- **Continued poor performance.** Not speaking up is not helping or being nice. Silence is also communication. Knowledge is powerful. Say it Now! is all about knowledge. Without it, there may be no chance for improvement.

- **Continued poor behavior.** Children and adults sometimes seek attention with bad behavior. No one ever challenges them, so they act out more. Sometimes just Saying it Now! jolts them out of their pattern.

- **Things get worse.** Take the previous bullets and imagine them getting worse. Silence is also communication. The problem is, it is open to misinterpretation.

- **Lost ideas, opportunities, products, knowledge.** How many great, groundbreaking, revenue producing, world-saving ideas are lost because someone didn't speak up? How many products were not invented or came to market that could make things better, faster, cheaper, easier, etc.? Put it out there. It either flies on its own, or grabs the attention of a manager, mentor, investor, or client that can make it a reality.

- **Stress**. Take any of the above. It can be stressful keeping ideas to yourself. Instead of enjoying the admiration of your boss, peers, or launching a new, exciting venture, you end up kicking yourself when someone else gets the credit for your brilliant (but unspoken) idea. There is stress in "what if?" It's stressful to remain in your present comfortable track when speaking up could change your life's course. Be brave enough to Say it Now! Say it Right!

- **Resentment and anger**. "I told you so," doesn't do anyone any good. When someone finally says something after you've been embarrassed, humiliated, made a fool of yourself, or destroyed a relationship, it's too late for a do over. Friends don't stand by and watch their friends self-destruct.

- **Poor or second-rate decisions.** You had a much better idea, or information that could have helped make a first-rate decision. Say it Now! Several things can happen. Your idea accepted as is, or goes through some changes, but the outcome is so much better. Or it's considered and rejected for any number of good reasons. Or some part of your idea is melded into another with a much better outcome. You learn more about how things work or what is valued and respected. You gain confidence just by speaking up.

> Friends don't stand by and watch their friends self-destruct.

- **Turnover.** People don't leave jobs as much as they leave managers. Have a good employee? Say it Now! Have some suggestions for improvement? Say it Now!

- **Loss of respect for leaders**. Leaders who don't Say it Now! leave their staff adrift. Who's steering the ship? I'm not talking about the micro-managing, dictatorial, "my way or the highway" kind of leader. A silent, say nothing, keep them guessing manager is just as detrimental to a team or organization.

- **Loss of collaboration.** Create a culture of Say it Now! without fear of ridicule or reproach. A good idea may turn into a great one with the insight of another person close to the situation or with past expertise.

- **Creating a culture of fear and/or dispassion.** Employees lose hope, feeling that the powers that be don't care. Employees take on a feeling of worthlessness – my ideas don't matter or aren't valued. "Why should I put myself out there? No one listens anyway."

At the time my daughter and I took our trip from San Francisco back to Maryland, there were incidents of big truckers targeting women drivers, ending in rape or murder. It was all over the news and women were warned to be aware that truckers often warned women drivers of trouble with their cars in order to get them to pull off the road. When the trucker started blowing his horn and trying to wave us over to the stop on the side of the road, I instantly thought he was "one of those" evil truckers and there was no way I was going to stop and be a victim. I assumed the worst, but he was only looking out for my safety. He seized the moment to Say it Now! the best way he could. I assumed the worst, but fortunately, things worked out and we made it safely off the road, put on the spare, and kept going. You can't control the outcome, but like that wonderful, caring trucker, do what you can to get someone's attention and Say it Now!

CHAPTER 5

SAY IT NOW!
Is A Tool In
The Box

In my home, I have one of those stackable plastic drawer units where we keep hand tools like screwdrivers, hammers, nails, tape, paint brushes – household stuff that is occasionally needed to make repairs or touch ups. It's easy to pull out the proper tool when needed. I may go weeks or months before grabbing a screwdriver to tighten a loose door handle or pull out a paintbrush to touch up a mark on a wall. I don't carry around a screwdriver every day just in case I see something in the house, neighborhood, at work, or in a place of business that needs tightening. My purpose in life is not to tighten up everything I see, just because I can. That would be time consuming, annoying, and inappropriate.

Say it Now! Say it Right! is a tool in your communications toolbox. It's not an occupation or an obsession. It's not license to give a running commentary or to judge everything and everyone you come in contact with. It's not an invitation to give unsolicited and unwanted criticism to everyone you know on any occasion.

> Just because you like hot sauce on your tacos or in chili, doesn't mean it goes well over ice cream or in your oatmeal.

Just because you like hot sauce on your tacos or in chili doesn't mean it goes well with ice cream or in your oatmeal. You wouldn't wear your work uniform every day, even on the weekends. True situations to Say it Now! and Say it Right! may be few and far between. You'll know when it's time if you are aware of two things: the situation at the time, and your gut feeling.

When I confronted Julie's dad, I knew that this was the moment, and if I didn't Say something Now! something terrible might happen. Did I read an article about that? Did I follow a flowchart of events that told me now was the time to speak up? No. I just knew in my gut and in my head that it was the right time. I couldn't keep silent. At that time, at that moment, for me, it was the time to pull out the screwdriver and start tightening that loose screw.

When my first husband was in the hospital recovering from some serious surgery, the doctors made it clear that they wanted him up and taking walks in the hallways as part of his recuperation. They put a walker in his room, and he walked with the help of a nurse for a while until they thought he was strong enough to take short walks on his own.

I visited every day at the hospital, and was aware of the doctor's orders, and tried to be as encouraging as possible. Day after day, I would come to his room, and he would be lying in bed, or sitting in the chair by the bed, with the walker pushed up against the wall. Despite the doctor's orders, he wasn't taking walks on his own. If I asked if he wanted to walk with me now that I was there, he would say no for a number of reasons. I'm too tired. I'll do it later.

One day I came to visit and the walker was nowhere in sight. When I asked where it was, he said that another patient down the hall needed it and he gave the walker to him. Now, if you've ever had a loved one who has had a serious medical problem and is recovering, you may understand the mix of emotions I experienced at that moment. I loved my husband and understood, as much as I could from the outside, what he was going through. I was also furious with him, because he was the only one who could do anything to recover from the surgery, get back his strength, and help the family regain some kind of normalcy and move on. His "good guy" actions were hurting him, me, and our family by prolonging his stay in the hospital and his return to the family.

This was the moment, the time to get out the screwdriver that had been lying in the drawer waiting for just this kind of situation. I could be "nice" and understanding and enable him to just lie there for whatever reason, letting his muscles weaken. Or, I could say what I thought needed to be said to motivate him to take charge and do what was necessary to get better.

I don't remember exactly what I said, but I ended with I wasn't going to come back until he got the walker back, did his walking exercise, and

> This was the moment, the time to get out the screwdriver that had been lying in the drawer waiting for just this kind of situation.

decided to rejoin the living and the family. I said I loved him, and then walked out, down the hallway and didn't turn back.

At that moment I wasn't thinking about possible reactions, or consequences. I knew I had to say something at that moment. To let it pass and say nothing would have kept things the way they were, prolonging the stress, anxiety, and frustration for both of us.

The next day I got a call from him. The walker was back, and he had just returned from a short, exhausting walk down the hall and back. In fact, he had walked down to see the needy patient, who had somehow gotten a walker of his own. They were now walking buddies. It wasn't too long before he was home, and we could get back to the task of putting our lives back together.

CHAPTER 6

SAY IT NOW!
For Leaders

The CEO in an organization where I was the HR Director would call me often to ask for help in tricky situations. I was his "go to" person whenever he had a wayward manager who needed some straightening up, or his guide when someone was beyond fixing and needed to make a quick exit. The problem was, while he knew that action was needed, he wasn't comfortable with confronting difficult situations. It got to the point that I was actually writing scripts for him to use when he had to fire someone.

His inability to Say it Now! in these situations had more fallout than just an employee who stayed too long in a job. It affected the people that he worked with who had to work with someone who was impacting performance and morale. His inability to Say it Now! at the right moments took a toll on the CEO, his staff, the entire management team, and the organization. His indecisiveness and inability to handle situations undermined his leadership and effectiveness. He was stressed by the situations and the knowledge that he was ineffective and wishy-washy. Trying to please everyone, he would agree with one person and then change his mind and agree with a differing point of view, leaving staff and employees confused and, at times, angry.

Employees are looking for leaders. Yes, the workplace is more collaborative. I hear it all the time when I ask applicants the question, "What is your ideal work environment?" Collaborative or collegial are the number one and two answers. Leaders who can't make a decision or who are always asking everyone else to make it for them lose credibility and respect. When things get crazy, employees want someone who will speak up.

Unfortunately, the team concept has taken over from strong leaders who were courageous to say what needed to be said without worrying about whose feelings were hurt or if they weren't liked or admired. I have always lived by the leadership mantra that people don't have to like me, or the decisions I make, but I want them to respect me and trust my decisions. Let's look at some situations where not Saying it Now! in a leadership situation affects the team and the leader herself.

> Leaders who can't make a decision or always ask others to make it for them lose credibility and respect.

1. **The impossible employee.** Most companies have one. The person who is a marginal performer, a total screw-up, or a miserable jerk who somehow escapes getting fired but keeps getting promoted up and out of one department to

another. Everyone knows he is worthless as an employee, but he's still there. Everyone concludes that he must have pictures of the boss in a compromising situation or knows where the body is buried (or the money is hidden). The inability to discipline or terminate the person – to Say it Now! diminishes the effectiveness of the manager, appearing weak, indecisive, and afraid to take charge.

2. **The meeting-hogger**. This is the person in a meeting who dominates the discussion, has loud side conversations while others are talking, or makes derogatory comments about every idea, subject or opinion. Equally annoying is the person who constantly checks her cell phone messages during the meeting and doesn't contribute anything to discussion. It's up to the leader to call out these spoilers and keep meetings on track.

3. **The "agree with everyone" leader.** This is probably the most frustrating. This leader agrees with whomever he is talking with at the moment. Unable to make his own decision, he listens to and seems to take a position on a situation during a meeting or conversation. The other person leaves that conversation thinking the problem is solved and the decision made. What he doesn't realize is the leader is going to do the same thing with the next person who has the same discussion, even if they have a solution 180 degrees from what the first person suggested. When the announcement comes out, there is confusion, disbelief, and a feeling of betrayal. The inability to take a position and stick with a decision is disastrous, for the leader's ability to lead the team and for the rest of the staff who have to live with uncertainty, lack of true leadership, and poor decisions.

Real leaders learn to listen to others. They have to. The CEO or manager can't be everywhere and needs the counsel and input from those who are making decisions at every level. But they also need to be able to make decisions and steer the ship in the right direction, despite opposing points of view.

The desire to please everyone is a downward spiral into leadership mediocrity. Instead of making the best decision on data, experience, and the counsel of those closest to a situation, the "pleaser" leader gives in to as many people as possible in order to keep the peace and make everyone at least a little happy. They chip away at the best decision with every concession. What was once a solid game changer is little more than more of the same. Leaders need to be able to Say it Now! once they have made a decision and go forward. Confidence is contagious. A confident leader who can make a decision, follow through, and then honestly assess the outcome with feedback from those involved or affected by the decision is inspirational and a mentor worth emulating.

Leaders set the tone for the organization. A company culture can be anything on paper, but the real culture of what is acceptable and what is not – how things are done, who has the power, and what is appreciated and what can get you fired – these things are more learned behavior. The leader is the head of the organization and/or a department, and he or she is always teaching by example.

> Confidence is contagious.

Organizations are made up of people. We look at diversity as having to do with age or race or sex, but the real scope is all that and all the employees' individual backgrounds, values, upbringing, financial situation, goals, dreams, fears, demons, and sense of right or wrong, whether innate or taught. Organizations also have policies, rules, handbooks, and other accepted ways of behavior, interaction, and accountability. There are unwritten expectations, like getting along with each other, cleaning up after yourself, working well with each other. Take all these variables – diversities if you will – and you've got a complex environment in which to accomplish the organization's goals and mission.

There will be many reactions and interpretations of meeting performance standards with so many diverse people. Not everyone is going to get along, work together well, or understand interactions in the same way. Leaders have to be able to understand and work with this incredible diversity in managing the organization through their senior team; just as they will in turn manage their direct reports and line staff.

The ability to Say it Now! for a leader is critical. If an individual for some reason goes against the accepted performance standards, is rude in her interactions, or blatantly refuses to follow instructions, the leader (or manager or supervisor) needs to Say it Now! People interpret their environment differently, and most of the time are unaware that they are off track. Let's be honest. There aren't a lot of brave, courageous leaders who want to handle difficult situations. An employee with broccoli in their teeth can go for weeks or months, committing the same indiscretion, without knowledge. Silence is also communication. If no one tells me that I'm difficult to deal with, then how am I supposed to know and do something about it?

> Silence is also communication.

When leaders lack the ability (or guts) to deal with a difficult situation, it continues and repeats itself. At some point, she will reach a tipping point and confront the clueless employee with a list of transgressions. Unaware there was a problem, the employee is stunned, confused, and maybe angry. He should feel deceived and disrespected as well. Had the leader addressed the problem early, the employee could have made changes and avoided the subsequent occurrences.

Who is responsible for the employee's poor performance? The employee, of course, for transgression #1 and #2. Transgressions #3 - #6? I vote for the leader. She had the opportunity (responsibility) to deal with the situation by coaching/counseling the employee to help improve his performance. For whatever reason, she allowed it to continue. The leader shares responsibility with the employee.

Growing up in a Catholic family, I learned early on about sin. It was the favorite subject of the nuns at St. Marks Catholic School. They made sure we knew about mortal sin (the hell fires were nipping at your heels – better go to confession before you die or you're on a one-way road to hell) and venial sin (get to confession; true remorse, a promise to never sin again, and a penance of a couple of Hail Marys or maybe a rosary will put you back in good grace). But there was another kind of sin, and it was the sin of omission. It was all about knowing the good that you could do but choosing not to do it. I'm sure other religions have their own variation, and religion aside, it's just common courtesy to alert someone of the broccoli in the teeth or an abrasive personality or a gruff manner.

I had the privilege of knowing and working with the most admirable, trustworthy, and professional Managing Director, Darren Smith. As Director of HR for Daufuskie Island Resort and Spa, I interviewed candidates for the top position and will never forget my interview with this gentle but remarkable leader. When asked about his leadership style, he said that he always wanted to be a "Force for Good." He had an incredible résumé and experience. Accolades, accomplishments, and raving fans as his references. But in my office in that interview, he wanted to be sure that I knew that his driving force, his core value, his mission as a leader, was to be a "Force for Good."

Leaders can choose their role. I remember the years that Darren Smith was Managing Director. It wasn't an easy job. But he held true to his values and mission. He never failed to Say it Now! and was a master of Say it Right! Leaders – speak up. You have a tremendous opportunity – and responsibility – to be a Force for Good.

CHAPTER 7

Recognize The Opportunities

I once heard a co-worker practice giving a presentation before she addressed hundreds of clients and potential customers. She was brilliant. She had great slides and commentary, but what was annoying was her repeated "OKs" and "Ums" when she talked.

After the presentation, the practice audience erupted in applause, stood up, and gave her a standing ovation. It was good, I thought, but it could be so much better.

As she was gathering up her notes, I hung back and made my way up to the podium. I complimented her on the points that I just outlined, and then asked if she would mind some feedback on the presentation. When she said she wouldn't, I suggested that she slow down, and be mindful of the OKs and the Ums. She was incredibly grateful (she's a gracious person anyway). The time to Say it was Now! at that moment. You can miss those moments if you don't act. When she gave the presentation the second time, she was brilliant and her delivery was much better (I told her that immediately after the presentation, also). The Say it Now! and Say it Right! goes for the kudos as well as the suggestions for improvement.

- Say it Now! when the moment arises. The best chance to be effective and get results is in the moment.

- Express your views from your point of view and perspective. The "I message" format expresses your opinion, is not accusatory, and doesn't make the other person defensive.

- Maintain the dignity of the person and his/her intelligence/ideas

- Come from a place of wanting the best for the individual, organization, project, process, and outcome. You don't always have to know your ideas or decisions are right, but they have to be genuine.

> The best chance to be effective and get results is in the moment.

What you have to say, or the decision you make, can actually get the results you want. Here are some clues it's time to Say it Now!

- **When asked**. One of the hardest things is to find an entrée to actually Say it Now! When asked, "Do you think I talk too much?" (and they do) or "Does this outfit look right for this interview?" (and it is horrible) you don't have to stress about finding an appropriate time to bring it up. Bam! You've been asked. You have permission. The right time is now. It would be wrong (and dishonest) to keep silent and say nothing.

- **Back burner issues.** You have witnessed your friend's boyfriend cheating on her. Or a co-worker keeps making simple mistakes on software that are easy to correct if you know one little shortcut (which you do). These are things that may

———

BAM! You've been asked. You have permission.

———

have been going on for a long time. Your friend probably is feeling stressed and embarrassed about her situation, afraid everyone can see how she lets herself be treated by the jerk. The co-worker may be oblivious to the mistakes or stressed out because he's getting flack for making so many. In both situations, Say it Now! At the least, your friend will see you as a pressure valve and find out just how good a friend you really are (now they have someone to talk to). Your co-worker will think you're the greatest mentor in the world (probably mention you in a speech when he wins employee of the year) and lose some stress over that mistake (one less mistake for him).

- **When observed.** You see something happening. Remember the screwdriver? I felt comfortable giving feedback on my co-worker's speech since I have done so with clients for years as an expert speech coach and evaluator. I risked the possibility of coming across as a "know-it-all" and overstepping my boundaries, since I'm not on her organizational level or even a close friend who could use friendship as a reason to comment boldly on her presentation. I do care about the organization, and my co-worker who had an opportunity to make the presentation of her life or miss the mark because of something she wasn't even aware of. To say nothing would be worse than risking putting her off by my comments.

- **When you're the expert.** A lot of people would like to think they are experts at everything. They have an opinion about everything and talk with such conviction that they want you to think that they are an expert. There are several things that make you an expert.

- o **You're the originator**. If you invented sippy cups, made the mold, and sold the first ones out of the back of your SUV, driving around the country, you are the expert. If you wrote the song, if you invented or created anything, you are an expert. You can speak with authority on the subject.

- o **You have the education or certification.** And you were paying attention in class, got good grades and passed your exams.

- o **You lived it.** You started a multi-million-dollar business with no money or prospects. Climbed to the top of Everest. Lived through the San Francisco earthquake (the big one). Ran the Boston Marathon. You've done it. So that makes you an expert. You are an invaluable source of information. Say it Now!, but be sure you also Say it Right! so you don't appear to be pompous and annoying.

- **When you're the leader.** (see chapter 6) You have to learn to Say it Now! to be the leader. People expect you to. They are waiting for you to say something, especially when the train is careering off the track.

CHAPTER 8

Speak Now, Or Forever Hold The Pieces (Of Your Life)

On my first wedding day, my father had the same little talk with me that he had with his other four daughters just before he walked them down the aisle. Talk about taking an opportunity. Just beyond the big double doors leading into the church were family and friends, waiting for me to start my walk down the aisle. Together in the vestibule of St. Mark's Church, my father let me know it wasn't too late to back out. No regrets. No shame. No kidding. He was serious. We could jump back into his car parked in front of the church and go back home.

How many times have you heard this pronouncement at a wedding?

"If any of you has reasons why these two should not be married, speak now or forever hold your peace."

I remember hearing this at my two church weddings. At the first, I would have liked if my sisters, whom I found out later had a lot of reasons why I shouldn't have gotten married, had spoken up, rushed the altar and dragged me away at the last minute. My biggest regret – in hindsight – I wouldn't have my exact, amazing children and subsequent grandchildren. The second time, I was warned the night before that I was making a huge mistake, but at that late date, the wedding was a runaway train on the track, speeding to its destination without my ability to stop it. Maybe I was the runaway train that wouldn't have stopped no matter how many people stood up, taking turns to give their reasons, and plead their case.

Speak Now! Say it Now! There is a sense of urgency in some situations, like in a wedding just before the bride and groom are about to make a lifelong commitment to each other before God and everyone. What other situations have the potential to become Say it Now! moments?

- A friend's husband (wife, boyfriend, or girlfriend) is cheating on them. Does the injured party need to know? This is a tricky one, because no one comes out the winner in this situation. Do they need to know? Knowledge is power, giving people the opportunity to make informed choices. Wait until you have the photos before you Say it Now! If you're wrong, bringing up the possibility of an affair can ruin the trust couples have built for years and alienate a good friend. Think about it, and then think again.

- A friend is in an abusive relationship and doesn't seem to think that the physical, emotional, or verbal abuse is anything to be concerned about. Need often trumps reality. Someone who doesn't want to be alone, feels unattractive or undesirable for any number of reasons, will hang on to even a bad relationship rather than risk being alone. Before your friend ends up in the shrink's office, the emergency room, or (God forbid!) the morgue, it's time to Say it Now! and fast!

> Need often
> trumps reality.

- A child who is into drugs, alcohol, promiscuous sex, cheating, bullying, sexting, skipping school, etc. No explanation needed. Be sure your information is solid. Consider the impact.

- A friend, or acquaintance, is too drunk to drive and you're a passenger. Register with Uber so you can call for a ride, or get a cab, walk home, etc. And take them with you. Take their keys. Do what you have to do to save yourself, your friend, and unsuspecting drivers who don't know they are on the road with a drunk.

- Someone is going to do something stupid (drunk or sober), like drag racing, or running a red light, or texting while driving. Yelling at someone while they are being stupid behind the wheel is OK. No time for caution or choosing words.

- A friend is killing herself with food, drugs, or alcohol.

- A friend, child of a friend, someone you know, is being sexually abused, harassed, stalked, or threatened with harm.

- Sometimes the "friend" that needs saving is you. We have opportunities at points in our lives where we need to speak out on our own behalf.

- Add your particular personal situation

The list could go on.

Sometimes a family member or friend will tell you something and then follow up with, "Promise that you won't say anything to anyone." You feel burdened with the information and obligated to keep silent. In some cases, it's **OK** to break the promise. Most of the situations above, depending on the nature of your relationship and the urgency of the situation, would qualify.

Sometimes the "friend" that needs saving is you.

SECTION II

SAY IT RIGHT!

CHAPTER 9

Now Be Nice...
SAY IT RIGHT!

Remember the story of the broccoli in my teeth? I was disappointed that my assistant had said nothing. But what if she had said within earshot of the audience, "You have something in your teeth!" I would have been equally disappointed and embarrassed. There are times when you have to speak up,

> There are times when you have to speak up, but you also have to know how to speak up.

but you also have to know *how* to speak up. That's what these Say it Right chapters are all about. You can always come from a point of your own feelings or perspective. For example, in this situation my assistant could have handled things in a number of ways.

- Say nothing (which is what she did). She saved herself the embarrassment of calling out a failing of her boss. By saving herself, she allowed me to go before a group of senior managers and unknowingly look foolish and unprofessional.

- Say with a laugh, shaking her head... "I can't believe it! You've got food stuck in your teeth. Didn't you check yourself out in the mirror? Can't you feel it?" This would have sounded accusatory, like, "Hey, dummy! Don't you know enough to check yourself out before you make a presentation?" A poor attempt at humor, which would be more humiliating.

- Say, "Maybe you shouldn't smile so much during the presentation. Keep it low key and serious. Too much smiling may make it seem like you think the material isn't important." That could be a back-door effort at keeping my lips stretched tightly over my teeth so I wouldn't show off the broccoli, saving me from embarrassment and her from having to confront the situation.

- Say, "I have to tell you that you have a piece of broccoli in your front tooth. I know you wouldn't want to go before this group and give your presentation that way. It could be embarrassing for you and distracting for the group." Straightforward and caring at the same time.

Now, what scenario is nicer? Saying nothing, or making an attempt to alert me to possible embarrassment? What someone may consider bringing up someone's faults, even if it's only in a particular situation, is the greatest act of kindness. Niceness. Caring.

Some of my best mentors were those who were bold and courageous enough to tell me gently about my faults. And some were not so gentle about it. Think

———

Think about it. Who cares more for you?

———

about it. Who cares more for you? Someone who will allow you to continue in your failings or faults, or someone who has the courage to point them out in a positive, caring way? Or steer you away from a detrimental habit you don't recognize but is affecting your professionalism and promotability?

I've found that most people are not even aware that they've got some kind of "broccoli in the teeth" situation. It could be any number of things. I once had a friend tell me that when I was relating a story in a presentation, my voice would gradually get softer and softer, making it difficult for him to hear. I never knew that I did this. I have probably been doing this for a long time, but no one has ever pointed it out to me. How many times have I given speeches, or spoken out in a meeting, or just had a conversation, and dropped my voice so low that others couldn't hear me clearly? I don't know because no one had ever pointed it out to me. But this brave soul, this kind friend, had the courage to point this out. To this day, I am careful to keep my voice steady and strong while speaking. It's a little thing, but to a speaker it's huge. He could have noticed it and just not said anything. I'm thankful for friends that care. Who take the time to be really nice.

When asked about his best friend, Jenny, Forrest Gump said that they went together like "peas and carrots." There are two components to being nice enough to tell someone what they need to know. It's the Say it Now! and Say it Right! These two should always go together, but as you will see in a future chapter, there are variations to these combinations. But let's look at how the two components could work together.

Here are some things to consider if you want to Say it Right!

- **Location**. Take the person aside, out of earshot of everyone else. If the situation could cause embarrassment, you can try to get the person in a private area before letting them know, because once you do, the first thing they will do is try to correct the situation, which can be even more embarrassing. If it's something that they may object to, or argue about, it's better to move out of sight.

- **Body language**. Say someone is giving an hour-long presentation in front of a group, just getting started, and you notice she has lipstick on her front teeth or he has ketchup on his face, or some other situation that needs to be remedied immediately. You could step to the back of the room, out of sight from the rest of the group, and try to give him a message using subtle charades. This is effective if you're really good at improv and he's on to your personal style of acting out situations.

- **Take a moment**. If he's already launched into the presentation, the moment has passed. Mention it at the first break, or if on Zoom, send a personal message via chat. He could then turn away from the in-person group or turn off the video for a moment and get things back in order. You certainly don't want to blurt out, "You've got lipstick all over your teeth" in front of the group.

When my children were little, I vowed that I wouldn't repeat my family's code of silence. I encouraged them to speak up, say what they needed to say, but to be mindful of the way they said it. I wanted them to feel they could tell me anything, and they did. Sometimes it wasn't the easiest message to hear, but at least we were talking, and I was aware what they felt or were dealing with in their lives. It's never too early with children, friends, or in any relationship to practice Say it Now! and Say it Right!

CHAPTER 10

Lots of Connection; Little Communication

One of my favorite songs is Paul Simon's "50 Ways to Leave Your Lover." It's the beat, the clever words, and the rhyme. But it's also the thought that there are so many ways to do something to solve a problem. "Duck out the back, Jack. Make a new plan, Stan. Drop off the key, Lee. Just get yourself free."

Today, we have 50 ways to communicate – email, texting, voicemail, Facebook, IM, Twitter, Pinterest, Websites, Skype, Zoom…and the list goes on. But are we really communicating?

One day, a friend and I were supposed to meet up after work. He was going to let me know where we were going to meet. I checked my email, and voicemail, but nothing. As it got closer to the end of my workday, I still hadn't heard anything. After calling his cell phone several times, and sending him a text, I still didn't hear back. Finally, I got a call from him, letting me know he was at a downtown restaurant, waiting for me. Annoyed, he asked, "Where are you?" I shot back, "Here, waiting for a message from you." He answered, equally frustrated, "I sent you an IM on Facebook this morning." Facebook!!! Who knew? We were making lots of connections back and forth, but no real communication!

Communication is a lot of things. It's sharing information. Digital communication can do the job, but it presents a set of problems.

First, just making the connection on the same digital media can be challenging and frustrating. Trusting an important message to digital media? Forget about the NOW! part of the message. Unless someone is staring at a cell phone screen, or as do some people, have it permanently attached to their hands at all times, they are going to miss that important, timely message.

The same for email. Once an email goes below the bottom of a screen, it's almost like it hasn't been sent. I get hundreds of emails each day, from work, and personal emails. They are all consolidated on my cell phone, so there is a jumble of real messages from real people and scores of unsolicited emails from cyberspace who happened to be snooping on my internet activity.

The second problem is that it can be misinterpreted, which can lead to all kinds of hazards. A harmless, informational message can come across as harsh, insensitive, or just plain uncaring depending on the words you use, mood of the reader, or the relationship between the two people involved. Connections are made but can also disconnect without the ability to ask questions, clarify, and discuss fine points in real time.

The third problem is the message is going to be flat and two dimensional without voice tone and body language. Even the "emojis" that are inserted into a digital message can't quite convey the subtle nuances of a turn of the head, lifted eyebrow, or crossing or uncrossing of arms that can change the entire feel and impact of spoken words.

By the time this book is published, the digital methods of communication mentioned may be obsolete, replaced by some newer, faster, sexier way of messaging. But the result is the same. Face-to-face is where a unique and personal type of communication takes place. Zoom, Skype, and FaceTime come close, but they still lack the ability to literally reach out and add the very personal element of human touch.

Face-to-Face is where a unique and personal type of communication takes place.

CHAPTER 11

SAY IT NOW! SAY IT RIGHT! Say It Face-To-Face

Face-to-face communications have the ability to not only communicate information but also the emotion that goes along with it. The point of Say it Now! and Say it Right! is to take the opportunity to communicate instead of just connect.

Standing up in a meeting to voice an opinion or share an idea has more impact and immediacy than a follow-on email after the meeting. There is no way to give your idea the same impact in an email as you can in person. Even if you send it to everyone who was in the meeting, you probably will miss a few who don't see the email. Also, each person is then going to interpret the message in a different way. There is no way for you to clarify or answer questions, or to plead your case. You've lost the immediacy and power of the opportunity to Say it Right!

Sending a text that says "I love you" with a smiley face may be cute and fun, but standing in front of someone, looking them in the eyes and saying "I love you" has the impact and emotion of all the fireworks going off over Australia's Opera House on New Year's Eve. In person, you can reach out and hold someone's hand. Touch his face. You get the idea. Now that's communication!

Reading this, you are probably thinking, that's scary. What if they don't respond in the same way? What if I make a fool of myself? That would be so uncomfortable. That's just not me! Say it Now! and Say it Right! takes a little courage and risk. That little girl who stood up to a big, tall, drunk adult may not have understood the danger, but did know she was taking a risk. Sometimes in order to be heard, you have to take a risk.

There was no internet or email when I made my statement to my friend's father, but what if there was? Would sending a scathing email afterwards, or texting him from the other room have been as effective? Would he have even seen the messages? Not everyone is as "plugged in" as you may be. If a digital message isn't acknowledged or returned, there is a whole world of miscommunication options to choose from, all left to the interpretation of the sender. Talk about risk!

In this digital age, we are connecting more, but communicating

_____

SAY IT NOW! SAY IT RIGHT! takes a little courage and risk.

_____

less. Say it Now! Say it Right! face-to-face gives communication on tough and tender messages immediacy, impact, and clarification. Immediate response is possible. No wondering what the message or motives are. The message comes with voice tone and body language. On-the-spot opportunity for question and answers. Response. Reaction.

Videos, Facebook posts, tweets, texts, emails (and whatever's the next digital method) live on forever in cyberspace and can come back to haunt you at any given moment. Face-to-face interactions and conversations are there for the moment. With so much being said (and recorded for all time) on social media and the internet, please, if you're going to Say it Now! – consider saying it face-to-face to Say it Right! Something that you Said it Wrong! can go viral, just as something you happened to Say it Right!

CHAPTER 12

Don't Text It Now! Or Email It Now! Or Leave A Voicemail Now!

If you want to know how to effectively use digital communications, you'll have to read another book. In order to live in this digital world, you have to participate on some level, and I'm no different. But there are some messages that don't belong on digital media at all. And some that should never go on Facebook. You may succeed in Saying it Now! through digital media (how more instant can you get?) but where you'll fall short is the Say it Right! part.

A friend of mine spent a lot of time on Facebook, and not just posting comments to friends' posts, but as a means of pursuing some of his favorite interests and many community and civic groups. He is not one to hide his feelings on any issue and was friends with some elected officials. One of his friends was a City Alderman up for reelection. The Alderman posted a comment about a hot issue contested in the election, and my friend posted a comment on Facebook, which was more of a question.

Now since I'm not on Facebook 24/7, I don't see his posts very often. But one evening, while watching the evening news, I heard the reporter talking about the race for Alderman and there on the TV screen was the post that the Alderman had put on Facebook. I looked up and saw, for a fleeting moment, my friend's name on a comment posted to the Alderman's post come up on the TV screen. It was just a flash, and I couldn't read the comment, but knowing his passion for politics, I hoped it wasn't anything he could be sued for or contained masked-out expletives! I stopped what I was doing, hoping to catch the story again. In the next news report, I was relieved when I saw the post again, and it was merely a question.

My friend didn't think his comment, posted to one of many posts on his friend's Facebook page, would end up as a visual for a news story on the evening news. Think about the posts, or text messages, or emails that you've sent that you thought were private. What would you do if you saw one up on the evening news for the world to see, or became a post that went viral, with thousands – millions – of hits on Facebook or Twitter?

One thing we've learned with the internet and social media is that it isn't private. We read stories daily about security breaches and identity theft. Something posted on Facebook goes viral, and it's not always the most uplifting and flattering message.

Some messages just aren't meant for digital, such as:

- Reprimands of any kind to anybody.

- Any response to a business or workplace situation with obscenities sprinkled like so much salt and pepper.

- Any response to a business or workplace situation with sexual or violent expressions, situations, or images.

- Relationship enders – "I'm getting a divorce," "I'm seeing someone else," I don't love you anymore."

- "You're fired" (or being demoted, or incompetent, etc.).

- Any kind of disciplinary action or counseling that has to do with poor performance that can lead to termination.

- Personal or revealing comments about someone else (friend, relative, etc.) that are either true or rumor.

Before you hit "send" or "post" or "tweet," look at your message and imagine it read by your mother, grandmother, boss, or best friend. Or on a billboard on your town's busiest highway. Or on the evening news. If you have the urge to Say it Now! choose the best way to Say it Right!

> Before you hit "send" or "post" or "tweet," look at your message and imagine it read by your mother, grandmother, boss, or best friend.

CHAPTER 13

If You're Going To Say It At All, For Goodness Sake, SAY IT RIGHT!

If you're going to start speaking up when the moment is right, you also have to learn to Say it Right! Blurting out whatever comes to your mind, no matter how important or powerful or strategic, can cause pain and confusion and dissention. There are several things to consider before launching on a Say it Now! mindset or leadership style.

When I decided to get serious about relaunching my speaking/consulting business, I found an online course presented by a well-respected and extremely successful professional speaker and marketing guru. I liked his open, honest style, and the content was just what I was looking for. Marketing was not my strong suit; in fact, I hated marketing because I was never trained on marketing and didn't like talking to people, trying to persuade them to hire me and asking for money.

When I launched my business in 1992, I was fortunate enough to meet some great people who liked what I did and referred me or hired me to do projects, training, and speaking. My business was basically all referrals, which was fine by me. I found that writing articles and a column in the local business magazine got me a lot of exposure with the right people, and I ended up on radio programs and as a regular "motivational expert" for a local CBS-TV affiliate every other week on the morning show.

I coasted along and went from referral to referral. Then, when 9/11 changed the world, I sought a safe haven and took what my mother would say is a "real job" with a paycheck and benefits, with a few dips back into consulting.

Now, after a few years, I felt the need to get back to my real passion, being an entrepreneur, on my own, pursuing my passions of communications, speaking, leadership, and writing. To make that shift, I couldn't rely on past relationships that had long gone. In addition, marketing had changed dramatically in the past 15 years, with digital marketing, websites, and social media which I knew little (or nothing) about.

If you want to be the best at something, find the best experts and follow what they have been doing that made them successful.

When I got the email from this expert, I signed up (he is really the master at marketing – I couldn't say No!) I particularly liked his humorous but no-nonsense style, amazing content with tips and techniques that anyone could put into practice. After our initial conversation, I was enthusiastic and ready to take on the course.

The course consisted of a number of modules online with two live phone sessions per week with other participants. We would discuss what was going on in our lives, what we were learning in the weekly modules, and then set goals for the next week in an "accountability session." The content was amazing and the phone calls with the other participants were fun and full of wisdom from their personal experience.

When I started the course, I told the leader that I had trouble focusing on what I wanted my business to be, and that I didn't have a lot of confidence, since I had been out of my own business for a long time. He promised to keep me focused, and for the first four sessions or so, I participated in the conversations, got some good feedback, set goals, and was progressing through the modules.

Then week five, I hit a wall, getting nervous about "killing my darlings" – speeches and programs that I really enjoyed doing but were no longer part of the new focus and brand. So, I found a domain name that was more generic sounding and more encompassing than the present one of "Say it Now! Say it Right!" so that I could include the new but not have to let go of the other programs that I really liked and were comfortable for me.

When it was my turn to contribute on one of the weekly calls, I announced the new generic domain name and my desire to continue with the new brand but still include other things under this new more generic domain name. Before I could complete the sentence, the leader stopped me in mid-sentence and went into a 10-minute lecture, telling me he hated the new name, I was basically a sniveling coward for abandoning my work and wanting to do a lot of "generic crap" and go backwards. I was stunned. Not so much as by what he was saying (which was spot-on true), and because I *was* getting cold feet and running back to what was comfortable and easy, but the way he was saying it.

The leader knew his stuff and is a legend in his field. I know that his message was intended for my benefit. He obviously felt that this was the critical moment to Say it Now! So, if all the pieces of the puzzle fit, why was I so uncomfortable being on the receiving end of honest, sincere, good advice? The message was the right one for me; however, it was shared "in public" with at least five other people on a live call. To me, it was the same as if we were all sitting around a table in the same room. He raised his voice and used strong, "absolute" language.

After it was over, I tried to make light of it, since I was so embarrassed that I was the object of this tirade. The others on the call didn't say much, except a few remarks to the leader about his rant. I was humiliated and horrified. I participated in the calls the next couple of weeks and heard remarks from some of the other participants like, "Oh, she came back after last week," referring to the lecture I got at the last session.

I continued to read the material and do the homework for the last two sessions but wasn't as enthusiastic about the online phone meetings. I listened to the exchange of the other participants, read the transcripts, and listened to the recorded audio of that fateful session once it was posted on the class private Facebook page. Even though the message was what I needed at the time (he nailed the Say it Now! part), I didn't feel compelled or excited to get back on the phone sessions and share my thoughts, not willing to risk a repeat performance.

After several weeks went by, I talked one-on-one with the leader in a private conversation, finished the course, and took several other webinars with him as well. He's a master at marketing, and effective in relaying information in a fun, informative, and easily understandable way. I needed a little tough love, and he seized the moment with his motives in line. In fact, the fearless leader of that online course, David Newman, of Do It! Marketing, is mentioned in the Acknowledgements section, and his endorsement is on the book cover. He's a great example of Say it Now!

The purpose of speaking out at the right time with the right message is awareness and possibility for change. What if you get the timing right to Say it Now! but you say it wrong? This situation happened with someone whom I didn't know personally, and never knew of before I started following him on Facebook and did some research on the internet. I knew he was an expert in Marketing, I liked his style, and delivery methods, and trusted that he offered a lot of valuable information that I needed to restart my business.

Sometimes the Say it Now! comes from someone you don't know well, or at all. In my years as a Human Resources Director, I read hundreds of résumés for all types and levels of jobs. One applicant in particular was extra persistent and becoming a pest. She made a lot of the common mistakes on résumés, and when she didn't get the job, she wanted some feedback. I sent her some direct and honest feedback, some of which could have been considered harsh, but she wrote back that she appreciated knowing what she did wrong from an "expert."

> Sometimes the SAY IT NOW! comes from someone you don't know well, or at all.

Help comes from unexpected sources. Don't discount advice just because you think someone doesn't know you well. David Newman took a risk to get through my fears. He has a lot to do with the fact that this book is entitled Say it Now! Say it Right! and not some boring, watered down title. Respect the source and take an honest look at yourself. If the comments fit the situation, have the good sense to take action.

Respect the source and take an honest look at yourself.

CHAPTER 14

Building a Culture of SAY IT NOW! SAY IT RIGHT!

Early in my consulting career, I landed a culture change project, headed up by the President of a Technical College. He was both loved and feared by his management team. Total Quality Management (TQM) was the latest management model sweeping business and industry at the time, and he hired me to transform the college from an autocratic "I'm the Boss" culture to one of customer-first thinking, collaboration, teams and quality systems and measurements. Aware that he was the biggest challenge in this transformation, he constantly looked for ways to encourage his team to speak up, disagree, and challenge him and his decisions to help him with his own personal transformation from boss to leader. What he created was a culture of Say it Now! and Say it Right! for himself and the team.

Leaders who want their organizations to grow, create new and better products and services, gain more market share, increase revenue, and improve employee engagement have to promote a culture that encourages and rewards Say it Now! and Say it Right! Smart leaders recognize that the people who do the jobs every day are the experts.

The front desk associate is an expert at customer needs, wants, and what motivates them to come in and purchase goods/services. They know what customers like and what they complain about – much more than a manager who interacts mainly with other managers or spends her time in an office in front of a computer buried in email and spreadsheets, or in meetings.

> Smart leaders recognize that the people who do the jobs every day are the experts.

Creating a culture of honest, timely information sharing, regardless of title, department, or seniority can have significant impact on making money, saving money, saving time, improving productivity, and customer satisfaction and loyalty. A leader can't know everything that's happening in an organization firsthand. He has to rely on the experts in his organization, and there are experts at every level, in every organization and discipline.

Want to know what the safety issues are in your organization? Where communications are breaking down? What the real morale or engagement issues are? Talk to employees at the front desk, on the production line, the loading dock, facilities maintenance, or in the cubicles. They can tell you where the issues are and what needs to be fixed.

Tips to Say it Right

It sounds good, but how do you build a culture of Say it Now! Say it Right!? Here are some tips to get started. And it starts from the top.

- **Say it!** Tell your employees that you need their honest opinions about topics. Encourage – no, mandate – employees to tell it like it is, while delivering the message professionally, with tact, and with making the organization better as the driving force.

- **Give permission for employees to disagree**. Encourage employees to express an opposing point of view.

- **Designate a "devil's advocate" at each meeting.** Appoint someone to deliberately look for opposing viewpoints to topics or suggestions. Have someone deliberately think of obstacles, pitfalls, and other things that would render an idea or process ineffective. Try to think of things that could go wrong. This is the time to bring these things up and have a discussion. Not after a bad decision has been made, or all possible problems haven't been considered and resolved.

> Encourage –
> No, Mandate –
> employees to tell it
> like it is.

- **Bring together the right people.** If the only people at your decision-making meetings or brainstorming sessions are managers, you're missing out on valuable information from subject matter experts – those who are closest to the problems, processes, systems, and people. Bring together stakeholders, especially at the earliest meetings. Stakeholders are those people who are closest to the problem, and those who are going to have to live with and carry out whatever decisions are made.

- **Retain your leadership option.** Honestly and earnestly consider arguments for and/or against solutions, and don't be afraid to disagree or override the group. The Say it Now! Say it Right! applies to leaders, too. After all, at the end of the day, the results of decisions are on your shoulders.

A Little Test

Identify a situation your organization is dealing with at the moment. It could be time for a company (department, work team) reorganization. Or an overhaul of your company's systems and processes. Whatever situation you choose, honestly answer the following questions. You can do this individually, or as a management team, work group, work team, or department. Pick and choose the questions to fit your particular organization, situation, or problem. Put the right people together for each question or situation, since the people who can solve a problem may differ by situation.

1. As a leader, what do you need to say? What decisions, pronouncements, changes, etc., have you been putting off? Has indecision or the reluctance to Say it Now! hurt your credibility?

2. What is keeping you from tackling the tough situations? Are you concerned about reactions from your team? If you start to be more decisive will you have a mutiny on your hands? Afraid key people will quit? When leaders hold back and let others make the decisions, or just abdicate and leave decisions unresolved, managers get used to assuming power and making decisions on their own. If this is your culture, taking back the leadership reins can be a painful and rocky road for all involved. Examine your own motivations. What

is the state of your leadership position?

3. What's the worst that could happen? The worst is allowing the broken culture to continue. What do you need to tackle first? Make a plan to begin establishing the culture of open, honest, timely communication.

4. Have you been Saying it Now! but no one is listening or you're making everyone angry and frustrated because you've been Saying it Wrong? Ask a mentor, trusted peer, or direct report to give you a straight and honest evaluation of your communication style.

_____

Make a plan to begin to establish the culture of open, honest, and timely communication.

_____

Make It Your Own

- What is your current situation?

- What message do you need to Say it Now?

- What is preventing you from taking action?

- What words or setting do you need to Say it Right?

CHAPTER 15

SAY IT NOW! SAY IT RIGHT! How To Deliver The Tender Message In The Workplace

Professional Situations – Saying Nice Things the Right Way

A company I worked with put together an employee recognition program that included comment cards that could be filled out by employees to give recognition to their co-workers when they did something over and above their jobs. The program started out saying things right, but quickly turned into a boring, repetitious, almost embarrassing ritual at the monthly all-employee staff meeting. Instead of specific accounts of extraordinary service or accomplishments, the cards were generic "you're awesome" notes.

Saying "nice" things at work to co-workers or the boss can be as tough as telling someone they have bad breath. In fact, for some it's easier to be negative than to give positive, honest, enthusiastic appreciation. It's not tough for the person on the receiving end. Everyone loves to hear how amazing they are. Children, parents, significant others, employees, and even the boss. There's a way to share the "love" that has the greatest impact.

OK, so you're not going to come into work one day and stare your boss in the eyes and say, "I love you." Well, maybe you have and it didn't turn out very well. If you say it to a co-worker, and they don't feel the same, you could be facing a harassment charge.

Everyone loves to hear how amazing they are.

There are times when you need to have a "tender" conversation or event in the workplace, like showing appreciation, recognizing an extraordinary sales goal, customer comment, major donation, or product breakthrough. Surprisingly, a lot of people are uncomfortable or unsure of how to say something nice at work.

There are a lot of reasons. You have to be careful in those tender or friendly situations that people don't take things the wrong way. You have to be sure you keep it professional and not cross the line by becoming too intimate or complimentary. Some people are so starved for any recognition and attention that they can misinterpret "good job" to mean "you're special" in a personal sort of way. It may sound far-fetched, but after 20+ years in the HR business, I've seen too many professional relationships take a dangerous slide down a slippery slope due to professional appreciation mistaken for personal attention.

Giving praise and recognition for a job well done is always appropriate. Unfortunately, it's often neglected or delayed – postponed for the annual performance review. Spontaneous expressions of appreciation are instead relegated to the monthly all-employee meeting. Or they are pushed off the agenda for more "important" things and never get recognized at all. Recognition should be immediate, if possible, or as soon as possible after the situation occurs, if it has to be delayed at all.

Recognition should also be specific. A thumbs up or "good job" in passing or in a meeting is nice, but to the person, it doesn't mean much. It can leave the recipient thinking, "Did my boss even know what I did? Was it significant? What was the effect on the team and company?" That type of gesture can come across as hollow and insincere.

To get the biggest payoff, for the person receiving recognition and for you as manager, co-worker or whatever, here are some tips:

- Be specific. Good job? What was it? Saying, "You went above and beyond customer service to the guests we had last week" is a nice comment but doesn't have the same impact as the following (a true story from my days at Daufuskie Island Resort).

  A couple were on their honeymoon, and the wife lost her wedding ring on the beach. When the distraught couple came to the front desk to report this missing ring, Amanda, one of the front desk associates, spent the afternoon searching the beach but couldn't find the ring. On her way home that evening, she rented a metal detector, brought it back to the resort the next day (her day off), and combed the beach. After hours of searching, she found the guest's wedding ring. When she handed it to the couple just before they checked out of the resort, they were ecstatic!

Why was it extraordinary? If you were Amanda's manager, you could say to her, "Losing a wedding ring on the beach on your honeymoon would seem like a terrible thing and impossible to even try to find. You took it upon yourself, without direction from your manager, to rent a metal detector and bring it to the resort to try to find the ring. Your efforts saved the day and turned a disaster into a happy outcome for the guests. There was no certainty that you would find it but were willing to try to make the guest have a positive experience."

What was the outcome? You continue. "The guests were so appreciative. They are going to tell all their friends and family about the resort's incredible caring staff and customer service. They have already posted the story on Facebook and Twitter. We have gotten lots of comments on the story and the kindness of the staff and resort. The couple already booked their first anniversary weekend with us next year."

Say thank you. Good things employees do enhance a company's reputation and have the potential for bringing in new customers and increasing loyalty with current customers. Let them know the whole story.

This formula for expressing recognition and appreciation can be used for informal recognition, performance reviews, and one-on-one coaching.

1. Describe the situation. What was the problem, dilemma? Who was involved? What was the setting?

2. Describe the action the person took to solve the problem. Be specific. Include all the things that they did in order to solve that particular problem, and what made their efforts extraordinary.

3. What was the immediate outcome? What were the details of the solution?

4. What was the outcome to the company, department, and organization? Delighted guests? Saved time? Saved money? Won a new client or customer? How did those involved react?

5. Say thank you. State why what happened was important. What gets recognized gets repeated.

Good things employees do enhance a company's reputation.

CHAPTER 16

Danger Zone: Watch Out For The Slippery Slope

Innocent professional attention, appreciation, and friendliness in the workplace, especially between (or among) the sexes, can be easily misinterpreted. Mutual admiration on a professional level can quickly take the slippery slide to confused and unwanted attention or to the wasteland of sexual harassment and stalking. None of these have any merit or place in a work setting.

When giving recognition, focus on the situation – not the person. What they did and how they did it – their actions – are what should be in the spotlight. "You are great! You're awesome. "You rock." All nice things to say but can be misinterpreted, especially when paired with:

- **Too much eye contact.** If you're gazing into someone's eyes for more than 10 seconds, it can be considered either aggressive or intimate. Watch the staring, especially if you're smiling or standing too close. These are signals that you're getting personal.

- **Personal comments**. "That shirt looks really great on you." "I love what you did to your hair." "That color really brings out the sparkle in your eyes." All nice comments, but a little too personal. Commenting on body parts or your personal reactions to another person's body parts is a dangerous path, full of opportunities for wrong turns. If you're complimentary on several occasions and then stop, the other person may feel slighted, or wonder why your attentiveness stopped. If you just can't stop complimenting people, direct your affection on someone close to you who really needs and appreciates it.

- **Touching**. A firm handshake (and quick release) is one thing, but holding someone's hand by cradling it in one hand with your other hand on the top for a long time, or holding someone's forearm, or putting your hand on someone's shoulder (and leaving it there while you're giving a 10-minute speech) can give the wrong message.

> When giving recognition, focus on the situation – not the person.

- **In private.** Giving praise, with any of the above thrown in and in your private office, with or without the door closed, is a misunderstanding waiting to happen. Give praise in public, out in the open.

- **Hugging.** I worked with a woman who always greeted you with her arms wide out, ready to give you a great big hug. "I'm a hugger," was her phrase, as if it were the same as being from a certain ethnic group or a part of the country. Hugging involves full body contact, and some people are uncomfortable with that especially if it is prolonged or repeated. Never in the workplace. And sparingly outside of it. You never know what the other person's needs, wants, or desires are. If you consider what prolonged eye contact can convey, a hug is eye contact on speed to some people.

- **Too much, too often**. If you are always finding private opportunities to praise one person, you may have to examine your own motives. Is it the great work they are doing, or a seemingly legitimate opportunity to get the person alone so you can have a special moment together? I said this was a slippery slope from both sides.

Giving recognition and praise is always the right thing to Say it Now! These are a few things to think about so you can also Say it Right! Done well, these "tender" workplace conversations can boost confidence and morale, and increase productivity and employee engagement.

SAY IT NOW! SAY IT RIGHT! In Action

CHAPTER 17

You're The Boss – Not Everyone Is Awesome

Just like Tom Hanks said in the movie *A League of Their Own,* "There is no crying in baseball," there is no crying at work. I once gave some constructive feedback to a new young employee of mine. I felt I was positive and offered suggestions for improvement. She burst into tears, feeling like she was criticized unfairly. Some people are unable to take even positive feedback.

Your responsibility as a manager is to get the work done most efficiently, within budget, and meeting company and strategic objectives. You are not running for boss of the year! It's not a popularity contest! Be fair, honest, and keep the best interest of your employees in mind. Being a good boss is offering employees a chance to stretch and grow…giving honest feedback to help them develop leadership and problem-solving skills and how to accept (and give) constructive feedback.

A lot has been written and said about different generations in the workplace. No matter what generation you belong to, the next one down the line can seem like they came from another planet and are determined to take over and ruin your workplace. Not so. Each has its own strengths and weaknesses. Play to strengths, and find out what motivates and engages your staff, peers, and co-workers, no matter what generation they are from. People are people, and a lot of 20-year-olds are old souls who don't like technology and some boomers have every digital device and sleep with their smartphones. Age, generation, and the other so-called markers that define people are interesting and can help explain why some people act the way they do. They can also prevent you from discovering the real person behind the charts.

> Be fair and honest and keep the best interest of your employees in mind.

Consider this situation – You're the new manager and inherited staff that have been on their own for several months before you were selected as the new manager. After several months of listening, talking, learning, and figuring out the job itself, you find that you've got some strong players and some weaker ones.

One staff member's only strength is she's outlasted everyone else on the team and has been in the same job for the last 20 years. One newer staff member with performance issues has been shuttled between departments over the past 18 months and has recently landed on your team. Two new young employees feel they are in charge, armed with confidence and brand-new masters' degrees. The final team member is strong and steady but is no match for the two young chargers.

Say It Now? Timing is everything

The present situation didn't happen overnight. Some is the result of years of not Saying it Now! – performance discussions, honest feedback, and action plans that hold individuals accountable. You may have this situation (or something worse) that you're dealing with now. You can ignore the situation, hope it gets better, pray for a miracle, or make a plan to deal with the situations. How do you handle it now?

1. As situations arise. No point in bringing in staff members one at a time in one afternoon to discuss their shortcomings. Let things happen organically. Expect the best. You're new to the team, not them. Take time to get to know your staff instead of creating unnecessary confrontation.

2. Performance reviews. Feedback, goal setting, and appreciation are expected – even welcomed at this time. You'll disappoint the employee if the review seems hurried, generic, and void of real suggestions for improvement.

3. One-on-one meetings with staff members to review project progress and outcomes.

4. Planning and brainstorming meetings.

Tips to Say it Right

1. Always reprimand in private and praise in public (when possible).

2. Address the situation or performance; don't attack the person.

3. Be clear about what you observe, and the gap between

expectations and present performance.

4. Stop talking and listen. Managers immediately follow up feedback with suggestions for improvement or some goals without taking the time to listen. Get the other side of the story. If an employee created the problem, give them a chance to solve it. When I managed a team, I insisted that when a staff member came to me with a problem, they also came with two possible solutions. Don't be a dumping ground for other people's problems.

5. Depending on the situation or the feedback, either tell the other person what specifically needs to be done in order to improve performance, with a timeline, or work out an improvement plan together.

> Don't be a dumping ground for other people's problems.

6. Affirm your confidence in the person's ability to improve performance and meet standards.

7. Ask what assistance or resources are needed to help the person succeed. Make it clear how you are committed to helping them reach their goals.

8. Be empathetic. Not everyone can handle feedback with grace and maturity. Wait out the crying or anger. Have a box of tissues in your office and within reach. Restate your position and reaffirm confidence in the person's strengths and commitment to make improvements.

Make It Your Own

- What is your situation?

- What message do you need to Say it Now?

- What's preventing you from taking action?

- What words or setting do you need to Say it Right?

CHAPTER 18

With A Peer – Don't Hold Back

Whether you're just beginning your career, or if you're a seasoned veteran, your progression up the ladder or status as an innovator or future leader depends on your ability to seize opportunities to communicate your ideas and thoughts in order to stand out from the crowd.

Situation – Your team of peers in the department works together well, but there is one person who is always late with assignments. She insists on taking the lead in meetings or presentations but isn't a polished speaker. She also doesn't research well, and the last report had a few errors which embarrassed the team.

Say it Now? Timing is everything

Before the next presentation or speaking opportunity, call a team meeting to honestly address the issues. Someone else on the team can take the lead, give the presentation, and fact-check the reports to make sure everything is correct. The team's reputation is at stake.

Collaboration takes respect and dependence on each team member to measure up. A manager's credibility, promotability, and leadership potential may very well depend on how they, or the team, take command of the weakest link and brings each team member to his/her best performance.

> Collaboration takes respect and dependence on each team member to measure up.

If you (or someone else on the team) fails to Say it Now! before the next opportunity, it's not the offender's fault for another missed opportunity. Say it Now! to make everyone look good and get your best message across.

Tips to Say it Right

1. If you're part of a team, this is a "we" situation. Frame your comments as part of the overall team effort, and then drill down to the specifics.

2. Avoid the "you" word, which makes your comments sound accusatory and the other person become defensive.

3. Here's a possible script for the situation. "We really blew it last time. We put a lot of work into the project, but the research was faulty and the points 2, 4, and 12 were incorrect. We need to do a better job of fact-checking the

work before going 'live' with the presentation. And Joe, I didn't see your usual excitement and enthusiasm for our conclusion and recommendations in your delivery. Did you have some concerns? For this next project, let's go over each part of the prep and presentation to see if there are any other areas that need work and fix them before the next Executive team meeting."

Make It Your Own

- What is your situation?

- What message do you need to Say it Now?

- What's preventing you from taking action?

- What words or setting do you need to Say it Right?

CHAPTER 19

With A Co-Worker – To Help, Not Hinder

When I finally went back to work full-time after my children were in middle school, I landed a job with Marriott Corporation at their headquarters in Bethesda, Maryland. After two years as an Executive Assistant to two Vice Presidents and a year in Consumer Affairs, I was recruited as a supervisor in the Benefits Department. Instead of helping me get acclimated to my new job, the other two supervisors did what they could to undermine my effectiveness with my new team. What I thought was helpful information from two seasoned supervisors was misinformation intended to make me look incompetent and force my team members to reach out to the other supervisors for direction.

As a newcomer, there is a point when you sit back and learn and another when you learn that others may not always have your best interest at heart. I always trust people have my best interest at heart (or at least aren't out to ruin me) until they prove otherwise.

Consider this situation:

1. A new co-worker is full of enthusiasm, but keeps interrupting during conversations, which is annoying his manager.

2. A front desk assistant is great at the computer system but rarely smiles at customers.

3. A co-worker ignores safety rules, with potential consequences to herself or other co-workers.

Say it Now? Timing is everything. When you notice it, as soon as possible after an occurrence, and always in private.

We are often our worst enemies. Most of the time, we don't even know it. If you've been in the workforce for a while, you've probably observed co-workers who do things (or don't do things) that can hurt their performance, credibility, or keep them off the promotion list that they aren't aware of. Call it coaching or mentoring. When your comments can help tweak their performance, add something to make it better, or stop them from making a career-ending mistake, it's time to Say it Now! and Say it Right!

> We are often our worst enemies. Most of the time, we don't even know it.

Tips to Say it Right

Here are some scripts to help you coach or mentor a co-worker. The comments should be short, specific, and done with the right intentions.

- "Joe, I used to work the front desk when I started at Luxury Hotels. You really have the check-in system down to a science. Lately, I've noticed that when there is a line of guests to check in, you get rushed and lose that great smile of yours."

- "I've seen how you drive that forklift in the warehouse like it was an ATV out on a racecourse. I'm concerned that you, or someone you don't see when coming around a blind corner, will get hurt. A warehouse accident with you at the wheel is not a positive for anyone."

- "I have to say something, and don't take this as a criticism. When in a conversation, you tend to interrupt when someone else is talking. It's frustrating for me when I'm talking to you, and others when we're in a group or in a meeting. I know you don't want to give this impression, and thought you might want to know, so your ideas and comments will be better received and considered."

A little humor can make feedback easier to take but be careful. Too much, going on too long, or the wrong voice tone can make good-natured humor seem like sarcasm or ridicule to the receiver. Stating your good intentions at the outset can help give your comments a soft landing and help the receiver save face and retain their self-esteem.

Make It Your Own

- What is your situation?

- What message do you need to Say it Now?

- What's preventing you from taking action?

- What words or setting do you need to Say it Right?

CHAPTER 20

With A Customer Or Client – Tread Lightly

The customers are always right...or are they? An encounter with a very assertive and professional airline desk agent gave me an excellent customer service story that I've used for years.

I used to travel all over the country as a contract trainer for an international business training company. It was the end of the week, and I arrived at the airport to catch my flight home. I went to the airline check-in desk and was informed that I didn't have a seat assignment for that leg of the flight. Worried that the flight was overbooked and I wasn't going to make it home, I tried to get a seat assignment. I was met with a smile and, "You can get your seat assignment at the gate."

OK. I was still worried but proceeded to the gate and was met by another very professional-looking gate attendant in her perfectly pressed uniform. She greeted me with a smile, even though she could see that I was a little worried. I asked for a seat assignment and she told me, "I can't give you your seat assignment at this time. About 10 minutes before the flight is ready to leave, I can give you your seat assignment. If you'll take a seat over there (pointing to a seat in the waiting area), I'll let you know when your seat assignment is available."

Now I KNEW that the flight was overbooked. I used some of my best tactics to get a seat. "The attendant at the check-in said you would give me my seat assignment when I got to the gate." The gate attendant smiled, and said, "Yes, I will be able to do that 10 minutes before the flight is ready to leave... (the rest of the above script.)"

That didn't work. No seat assignment. Next – "I know that this flight was overbooked. I have a confirmation number, and I want a seat assignment so I'm sure I'll get on the flight." Same smile, same calm demeanor from Ms. Professional Gate Attendant. Same message prefaced by the honest affirmation that yes, airlines book more seats because statistically some people don't show up, but she assured me that I would get my assignment...yes, you guessed it, "10 minutes before the flight is ready to leave." I tried, "I'm a Medallion member," "I fly over XXX miles a year" – just about everything I could think of. She never got angry, never lost her smile. She answered every objection I threw at her, pleasantly, and then just repeated the 10 minutes' speech, and please have a seat. After the last one, I started to laugh, and said to her, "You're really good at this." And she was. She knew how to Say it Now! (No, you're not getting your seat assignment now) and Say it Right! (with a smile, calm demeanor, respectful language, but assertively).

What about these situations?

- A regular customer is giving you a hard time about waiting too long for a special order to come in.

- A prospective client is ready to buy but wants to haggle about your fees.

- A customer is verbally beating up one of your employees, using expletives and aggressive, threatening body language.

Say it Now? Timing is everything. Employees need good pay, comfortable, safe working conditions, and recognition. They also need a manager or supervisor who looks out for them, supports them, and "has their back" in tough situations.

Tips to Say it Right

1. Loyal customers value the friendship or inside track that they feel they have with the "owner." Take them to lunch or meet for coffee like friends would do. Say you value your friendship, but you are uncomfortable when the "friend" relationship spills over into business. You want to keep them as friends but need to keep business transactions separate.

2. Working with customers or prospective customers is tricky. On one hand, you want them to be customers for life, repeat offenders. So, you can take some annoyance and demands. But there is a tipping point – and I don't mean a few dollars added to a check – where you've had enough, or an employee has had enough (justified). Step in and take the heat off the employee. Solve the problem first, and then

use the situation as a learning experience for employees on handling difficult customers in similar situations.

3. You charge a fair fee for your extraordinary, awesome products and services. If you don't think so, and are willing to cave in at the slightest resistance, why should anyone agree to pay the asking price? First of all, examine your fee structure. If it's really fair for what you deliver, stand firm. Or give a base fee for the minimum and offer add-ons for additional fees. People love options because it gives them a choice and a feeling of control. Some prospects are just jerks and will try to knock you down because they can't pay or it's just part of the negotiation game. After you make your case, or lay out the options, stand firm. Some business and clients are worth walking away.

4. Repeat business is golden. Clients or customers who feel friendship makes discounts an obligation on your part aren't so shiny. Ditch the guilt, and make a small concession if you like, but if you don't value your work, or don't feel you deserve the price or fee, rethink it. In the end, you may lose a customer, but retain your own self-esteem.

> Some business and clients are worth walking away.

5. Employees are paid to be nice to even the worst customers. They can't be forceful or direct to a customer, but you can. They want you to rescue them and "have their back." Take the offending customer aside if possible, but if not, speak clearly, assertively in a clear, steady voice. Your job is to redirect the customer's anger so it is focused on the situation and not the employee. You can deal with any blatant poor customer service later with the offending employee. The immediate Say it Now! message to the customer using rude,

demeaning, or abusive language with an employee is it will not be tolerated.

Make It Your Own

- What is your situation?

- What message do you need to Say it Now?

- What's preventing you from taking action?

- What words or setting do you need to Say it Right?

CHAPTER 21

Managing Up – SAY IT NOW! SAY IT RIGHT! To The Boss

How do you say no to the boss when she delegates another project when you're already overwhelmed? What if you disagree with a decision she made that affects you and your peers? Or you are asked to do something that is unethical or illegal? Or you have a better suggestion that is opposed to your boss's objectives?

Who hasn't felt that way at one time or another? A lot of job dissatisfaction, frustration, and stress come from feeling trapped and unappreciated in a job by your boss, co-workers, and peers. No matter what your position, title, grade level, or pay rate, you can say what needs to be said and be heard. There are risks and rewards, and you have to find your comfort level with both. Weigh the risks against the rewards. There are risks and rewards when you Say it Now! There can be greater risks and rewards if you keep your head down and remain silent.

Managers aren't always chosen because they are incredible leaders and have it together and know how to get things done. People get promoted because they have the skills or smarts to do the job. Some get promoted because someone wants to get rid of them – they are the lesser of two evils, they are a warm body in a crisis situation, or they have pictures of the boss in a compromising situation. Sometimes they are rude, clueless, and don't have the skills necessary to do the job. They may have poor communication skills, are uncomfortable with people, and aren't very friendly. So, why be concerned about speaking up? Especially if it's something that your manager needs to know.

Whistleblower laws protect employees who speak out when the boss or board or executive team is cooking the books, embezzling money, or any other moral, legal, or ethical infractions. That's the way it is supposed to work, but it's still a big risk. Depending on the company, the people involved, and whether or not it's a slow news day, it can make the local papers, the evening news or CNN. Protection aside, you may still lose your job, or will be so uncomfortable that you'll leave on your own under the pressure from the boss or your peers. You may end up being a hero, but a hero without a job.

"If both of us always agree, one of us is unnecessary."
Dale Carnegie

Smart managers hire people that are even smarter than they are, or at least smarter in areas that they are weak. In those cases, they are even smarter if they listen to those smarter people. You can "manager your boss" easily if you're one of those smarter people. The key is to earn your boss's trust. Make it clear, in word and deed, that your main objective is to make him/her look good to his boss and the rest of the organization.

Unless your boss is really a bonafide crook, and you're obligated to turn him over to the authorities, you should have his back. Give him the same respect and support you expect from him. You can help by intentionally giving the other side of a situation, taking an opposing view, just to bring out any roadblocks or objections before someone else does. Help your manager look good to his manager and everyone wins.

> Help your manager look good to his manager and everyone wins.

Sometimes, working for someone who lacks good management skills can be frustrating. Consider the following:

- Your boss is overwhelmed with work but doesn't delegate projects.

- Your boss only talks to you when you've done something wrong and never gives praise for accomplishments.

- She is indecisive and it's dragging down morale.

- People are afraid to speak up in meetings or disagree with the boss because they get humiliated if they do speak up.

Say it Now? Timing is everything. As soon as possible after a situation.

Tips to Say it Right – some phrases to get the conversation going.

- "I've observed…"

- "I don't mean this to sound critical or complaining, but there is something that concerns me and I'd like to get your thoughts on it."

- "You probably aren't aware of this, and it's probably not a big deal. I've noticed…" The reason I bring it up is your presentations are powerful and have a lot of content, and this _____, in my opinion, is taking away from the overall impact."

Maybe your boss has a habit of rubbing his left ear when he talks. I remember watching a video of one of the world's top motivational speakers and best-selling authors. The principles he shared were groundbreaking, but he constantly licked his lips, the top and bottom, while he was talking. Reading his book or listening to an audio version you'd never know he had this annoying habit. But watching it was so distracting and, for me, took away from his message.

I often wondered if anyone else noticed, and why someone didn't Say it Right! while he was filming the video. What a difference it would have made in his presentation if someone had the courage to say something – I can't imagine a professional speaker of his caliber would be offended by honest, sincere feedback. Videos can live forever on YouTube, repeating an embarrassing moment or a poor performance to a global audience. Be kind and Say it Now!

Your boss may appear to be a superstar, but regardless of who she is, if she's licking her lips constantly, or twirling her hair, or constantly late for meetings, or doesn't return emails, she needs to know. For her sake and the sake of the team.

Bosses who won't delegate are dealing with their own issues, such as:

- They don't know how to delegate.

- Delegating in the past was a disaster.

- Teaching someone how to do something takes more time than it's worth, and often the result isn't as good as doing it yourself.

- The boss is afraid someone else can do things better and will show them up.

- They want all the praise for getting things done.

- If the delegate screws up the project, the boss has to take the time to do it right and then do damage control.

- They get some weird satisfaction from being overwhelmed and getting attention.

The Reluctant Delegator

It's stressful on the whole team when projects are delayed or handed out at the last minute (robbing anyone of a good result). Here are some tips to win the trust of a reluctant delegator:

- Ask for a chance to do a project. Frame it as professional development.

- Set up a follow-up schedule so your boss still retains some control but lets you do the project.

- Don't insist on top billing. Let the team get the credit. Assure your boss you're not out for personal glory but to help make him and the team look good.

Gain the confidence and respect of the boss and watch more opportunities come your way.

Some More Tips:

- Be proactive and volunteer for a project that your boss needs to delegate and will help you gain valuable skills and experience. Before you ask for a meeting, put together several points on your experience, skill level, potential for improved performance, productivity, or professional development fits with the project.

- Remind the boss how taking a project off her hands will free her up to do more pressing, higher level projects.

- Start complimenting your boss when he does something worthwhile. Bosses are humans, too (really!). They probably don't hear much praise from their boss, either.

- Find something they do well, or a leadership trait you admire, or an idea or project that went well. Managing up means being a good example and mentor to your boss without being preachy or teachy.

When your boss gives you a compliment, don't blow it by saying something like, "Oh, it was nothing," or "Don't mention it." Learn to take a compliment. If you don't, you negate the comment and the effort of the other person. What gets rewarded gets repeated, and your simple, "Thank you, I appreciate it" validates your boss and makes him more likely to repeat the kind words at another time.

She's indecisive, and it's ruining morale.

Leaders are supposed to make decisions. They have the title, the authority, and the responsibility to make decisions. Now, they don't have to be autocratic, making decisions without any input from their staff, other employees, peers, or stakeholders. But after getting input, analyzing data, soliciting ideas through brainstorming sessions, and testing and measuring possible alternatives, leaders are supposed to make decisions and stick to them until proven otherwise. This gives some stability to the team and assurance that someone knows what they are doing and is going to be accountable for the decisions. Wishy-washy leaders put stress on the entire team through indecision, lack of belief in their abilities, and the outcome of their actions. Say it Now! When your boss makes a decision, express your support. Applaud them for making a decision and take action. Nothing says I support you and agree with you like putting a decision into action.

Some tips:

- When your boss does make a decision and it's within your authority, act on it. It's difficult to waffle when things are already in progress. Managers need encouragement and praise, too.

- Congratulate your manager on her brilliant decision and give it your full support. Remember, what gets recognized gets repeated, no matter what rung of the ladder a person happens to be standing on.

People are afraid or reluctant to speak out in meetings.

First of all, if you're invited to take part in a meeting, you're expected to contribute. If you have an idea or a comment, take the opportunity and Say it Now! Raise your hand, take the microphone or the floor – whatever the process is. You can use some of the opening phrases as in talking to your boss. One of my managers would invite people to meetings as long as they contributed. If she noticed that someone was just occupying space (or staring into it) during a meeting, they weren't invited back.

Say it Right! If you think the idea is good enough, or your comment is relevant or compelling, it's important enough to mention. Examine your motives. To have your comments considered and recognized, go easy and stick to the subject. "You're wrong" or "That won't work" are "all or nothing" phrases that predict an outcome you can't possibly be certain of. Plus, they attack the person instead of the idea. If you are certain someone is wrong, then back it up. If you have a better idea, put it out there. If you don't, the next great idea, like the cell phone or backpack or Chia Pet will never become reality. It may not be as great or groundbreaking. But it's yours.

Some tips:

- If your manager calls a staff meeting to go over the work of the past week, or looking forward to the next week, this is the perfect time to speak up. If staff members have time to report on their own thoughts, or challenges, it's another opportunity to Say it Now! Brainstorming sessions are golden, because one of the "rules" of brainstorming is to not judge any ideas. Take everything as it comes. You can introduce your ideas or thoughts without fear of instant criticism and rebuke (if everyone follows the rules).

- If a staff meeting isn't appropriate (or is the risky place that no one wants to speak up) then take an opportunity to talk to your boss one-on-one.

Make It Your Own

- What is your situation?

- What message do you need to Say it Now?

- What words or setting do you need to Say it Right?

- Risks? If you Say it Now?

- Rewards?

CHAPTER 22

Hire Me And You Won't Be Sorry. SAY IT NOW! SAY IT RIGHT! In A Job Interview

If you're desperate to get a job, and are lucky enough to get an interview, you may want to say anything and everything that you think the interviewer wants to hear or that you want to say. Interviews can be tricky.

Think about what you're doing in an interview. You're trying to figure out if this is the place where you want to show up five days a week, eight or nine hours a day. You want to find out if you want to work with these people, report to this prospective boss. You may really need a job, but if you say the wrong things just to get an offer, you may be in for an even bigger disappointment once you're on the job.

Job interviews are the time to be excruciatingly honest. Honest about yourself and your abilities. Your likes and dislikes. Your past experience, the depth of your knowledge, and what you don't know. Put all your cards, as they say, on the table.

> Job interviews are the time to be excruciatingly honest.

Zoom or Skype are great ways to interview promising applicants "in-person" who can't, because of time or distance, make it in person. I once interviewed a young woman for a position on Skype, and it went very well. She was poised, responsive, energetic, and highly qualified. We offered her the position, and I emailed her an offer letter and a copy of our employee handbook. A couple of days later I got a call from her, saying she had a question. She read through the employee handbook and noticed that our personal appearance code ruled out visible tattoos. She was concerned because she had a few that would be visible. With the magic of smartphone cameras, she sent pictures so we could make a determination and everything worked out. Not only was she qualified, but she was also honest and took the risk to Say it Now! about her tattoos before she arrived on the job. That characteristic goes a long way in a job interview.

Once you get a job, it's too late to Say it Now! In my years as a Human Resources Director, I've had new employees, on their first day on the job, ask if it is too late to ask for a higher salary, different work hours, a better office, or a different title. It's not as if they didn't have an opportunity to discuss these issues in the interview.

The last question in any interview is always for the applicant – Do you have any questions for us? That is not a rhetorical question. Every applicant should have a list of questions. If you didn't come in with any, take notes during the interview and ask away at the prompt. If you don't have any questions, it will seem that you haven't thought very hard about the job or didn't research the company or you're just not very skilled at interviewing. If your inner antennae go up during the interview and you have a question, write it down and ask it at the end of the interview.

Of course, you don't want to ask how soon you can get a raise, or when you can take your first time off. You can get that kind of information, but that comes under the category of Say it Right!

> Every applicant should have a list of questions.

Say it Right!

Here are some questions to avoid, and some ways to Say it Right! in an interview to get the information you want.

1. When do I get my first raise? Instead of saying this, you can ask, "What is the process for performance reviews?" or "What would it take to get an 'excellent' rating for this position?"

2. When can I take my first vacation? This makes it look like the first thing on your mind is not being at work. Instead, you can ask, "What is your time off policy?" If you know that you have a two-week vacation scheduled that you can't (or don't intend to) cancel, the time to mention it is during the interview, and just Say it Now! Don't think that you

can wait until you've nailed the job and then mention the vacation. Saying it Now! is Say it Right! in this instance.

3. What is the pay rate for this position? It's amazing to me that candidates don't ask this question in an interview. If you're not clear what the position pays, or whether it's hourly or salaried, or how often you are paid (so you can schedule your finances), you should ask those questions in an interview. Unless you're working for free, or are independently wealthy, salary or hourly rate is one of the most important factors for considering a job.

Before you start your job search, clean up your digital presence – Facebook posts and friends. Twitter. Instagram. Join LinkedIn and use the tutorial to set up a professional profile. Consider changing your voicemail message and email address to just your name at gmail. com. What you're linked to can either help or hinder your first impression.

> What you're linked to can either help or hinder your first impression.

Make It Yours

- What is your situation?

- What message do you need to Say it Now?

- What words or setting do you need to Say it Right?

- Risks? If you Say it Now?

- Rewards?

CHAPTER 23

With Your Kids – I *Am* The Boss Of You! Listen Up!

When my daughter was a junior in high school, she moved to the beat of her own drum. She was gorgeous, fun, had a wide group of friends, and was a little rebellious, too. We were loving parents and busy. Both her father and I had demanding jobs with commitments to church, activities, and hobbies. We figured since the kids were old enough to drive, had jobs, and were responsible, they could pretty much take care of themselves. Our son was two years older and attending Purdue University in Indiana. We had settled into what we thought was a happy family routine.

Spring break was coming up, and all my daughter could talk about was the trip to Ocean City, Maryland, that she and some of her friends were planning. Ocean City was only a couple of hours drive on the Atlantic Ocean, and she had made arrangements to be off from her part-time job.

The weekend before her trip, she and her best friend went to a party, and like a responsible child, she was home before her 11p.m. curfew. But something was funny. She came into the family room with her friend and plopped down on the couch. It didn't take too long before we could tell, from her slurred speech and repeating herself, that she had been drinking. The more she talked, the more we were convinced. Even her friend tried to stop her constant chattering.

After asking her friend to leave, we confronted her. We were disappointed. She's underage. She wasn't driving, but in her state, she wouldn't have had the presence of mind to avoid any number of dangerous situations. Her punishment? The trip to Ocean City was off.

Talk about tough love. She was shocked and angry. She cried and pleaded for mercy. We were steadfast. This was the time…the moment – to Say it Now! For the next week, she sulked, stayed in her room, only leaving to go to work and get food from the kitchen. I don't know who suffered more – my daughter or her father and me. Years later, we talk about that incident, and the impact it had on her life. It had a profound impact on ours, too. Someone has to be the boss in the family, and like it or not, sometimes it has to be you.

> Someone has to be the boss in the family, and like it or not, sometimes it has to be you.

Say it Now…

In this situation, the facts were right in front of us. Before you confront your kids with possible behavior problems, get the facts. After a certain age, kids don't like to confide in parents, especially if it's something they feel their parents won't understand or approve of. Accusing your kids of something they aren't a part of can do more harm by making them defensive and destroying trust. Lose trust, and you lose your line of communication.

Not confronting kids if you think they are into something that is harmful, destructive, dangerous, or illegal is irresponsible. No parent likes to be faced with the possibility that their little darlings may be going down the wrong path, or leading others astray. If you do suspect or have reliable evidence, it's better to confront it early, before things go too far. Better to have a confrontation, argument or even a few slammed doors, or screaming fits than a knock on the door from the police.

> Lose trust, and you lose your line of communication.

All families have rules and values. They have beliefs and expectations. Do your kids know your family values? What will and will not be tolerated? Most of the time, these things aren't written down, like the rules of the road, but they should be expressed and demonstrated in such a way that everyone understands what's acceptable and where the boundaries are.

Kids need boundaries for their own protection. Look both ways before crossing the street. Put the milk back in the fridge so it doesn't go sour. Don't put your backpack on the floor where someone can trip on it. Say "please" and "thank you." These are simple illustrations but make living together a pleasant experience.

You have to Say it Now! to stop the runaway train in its tracks and Say it Right! to get your message across. Here are some tips to

Say it Right!

- Ask questions. Things aren't always as they seem. Before you make a statement, find out what's going on. Use a friendly tone. This is not the inquisition. Even in court, a person is presumed innocent. Better to clear up a misunderstanding than close off vital future communication.

> Better to clear up a misunderstanding than close off vital future communication.

- Verify. Think your child is skipping school? Call the school office to see if they have been handing in "sick notes." Missing work? Ditto. Taking drugs? If you've checked off all the boxes for warning signs, and have ruled out a medical condition, this can be an option. This is a tough one, but you can get a test kit and clear up any doubts.

- You've heard the same story from several sources. Your child visits a friend's house and things go missing. There could be a lot of explanations. The second or third time at the same or another friend's house is a signal to start asking the right questions.

- Make your house the "cool house." The best way to know your kids' friends is to have them in your home. Now, you're not going to be part of the crowd, but you can see and get to know the kids and their parents (if they drop off or pick up their kids at your house). Keep your distance and be the parent (out of the way) but keep your eyes and ears open.

> Make your house the "Cool House."

- Talk it out. Little kids may need to have their hand pulled away from an electric socket if they get too close, but you can still show respect for them by explaining why they shouldn't touch a live electrical socket. Children need respect, love, and care at all ages. When they stumble, be there to gently pick them up. Make correcting the situation their responsibility. Help them make a plan and give little tough love, but never respond in anger or with physical, mental, or verbal abuse.

This may sound like you're snooping on your kids. Maybe it is. I'm not just talking about teenagers. Kids pick up values and habits at all ages. Be sure your kids know what your family values are early and be ready to "be the parent" when the situation arises.

Make It Yours

- What is your situation?

- What message do you need to Say it Now?

- What words or setting do you need to Say it Right?

- Risks? If you Say it Now?

- Rewards?

CHAPTER 24

The Time To Be Silent

"Turn, Turn, Turn (To Everything There Is A Season)," was a popular song written and recorded by Pete Seeger in the late 1950s and covered in the 1960s by the Byrds. The lyrics were taken from the Book of Ecclesiastes (3:1-8) in the Bible. The passage says there is a time and a season for everything, and, among other things, that there is a time to be born and a time to die; a time to mourn and a time to dance; a time to be silent and a time to speak.

This comparison phrase became very real to me when my son was in high school. When I was a teenager, I had a bad case of acne. I tried everything available at the time to cure and cover the spots – Clearasil, Cover Girl pancake makeup, applied in layers, bangs to cover my forehead. My mother, who suffered with me, bought Ponds cold cream, oatmeal soap, and even surgical soap to dry out my skin and hopefully make things better. They only made things worse. It got to the point where I didn't want to go to school at all. In my family, a case of acne, while disturbing, was considered just part of growing up and something where you did what you could and endured the rest until it ran its course.

Whether it's genetics, or just part of growing up, my son went through a similar bout with acne as a teenager. This time I was the parent and was determined that my child wouldn't go through the same thing that I did. We tried the latest topical treatments and cleansers at the time with little success.

Now my son wasn't as distressed as I was about this. He was a cool, calm kind of kid, much like his father. I, on the other hand, was a little more frantic. The "fixer" in the family, I suggested making an appointment with a dermatologist.

The day of the appointment, we went to the dermatologist's office, and while my son was sitting on the exam table, I started telling the doctor about the situation. The doctor turned to my son and asked a question, and I promptly answered it. After a couple of times with me intercepting the questions, the doctor stopped, looked at me and said, a bit exasperated, "Ma'am, I think your son can speak for himself."

The doctor saw his moment to Say it Now! Here was my teenage son, who was the one with the appointment, and I was being an overbearing mother, speaking for him when I should have stepped back and allowed him to speak for himself. "A time to be silent and a time to speak." I have told this story many times over my speaking career. At that moment, a light went on. I needed to be silent and let him take charge. There is a time when as parents, we need to stop speaking and doing for our children and allow them to speak for themselves, deal with life situations, and figure things out for themselves. The parenting "helicopter" needs to land and go into the hangar. Power down.

There are other instances when it's time to be silent. Some managers use parenting techniques instead of leadership skills to get things done. Micro-managing employees looks a lot like helicopter parenting moved to the workplace. Managers may be reluctant to delegate to their staff because they might make a mistake or not do it the way they would. Or they are afraid that the employee will fail, and then everyone will look bad. If a manager has been

> The parenting "helicopter" needs to land and go into the hangar. Power down.

Saying it Now! with timely coaching and skill development and Saying it Right! by clear, honest communication with the purpose of building up confidence and an opportunity for success, there comes a time to finally be silent and let an employee make it (or not) on her own. There is a time and place for parenting, and it's not between adults in a work setting.

Early in my consulting career, I worked on a quality system project for a major chemical manufacturing company for about 15 months. During that time, I was on site just about every day, and often brought my lunch and kept it in the company's break room refrigerator. Everyone in the plant used the break room and made it clear that everyone was responsible for keeping it clean. There was a cleaning schedule on the refrigerator door, listing employees who were responsible for cleanout every Friday. There was also a sign hanging over the sink area that read, "Your mother doesn't work here. Clean up after yourself." There comes a time when parents and managers and coaches and leaders have to stop talking, keep silent, and let others take charge of their lives and responsibilities. "For everything there is a season (turn, turn, turn)." Saying it Right! can mean a time to stop saying anything else. Your turn is over, and it's time to give someone else the stage.

Some of my best and most beneficial lessons came from making and recovering from mistakes I've made. You could probably think of a few lessons well learned from your own mistakes. Making them, and going through the process of recovering, was often painful, but they made me stronger and more confident and gave me a sense of my ability to handle difficult situations and come out stronger and better. Overparenting, whether it's your children, employees, friends, spouse, or co-workers, robs individuals of their own opportunities for self-discovery and growth.

_____

"Your mother doesn't work here. Clean up after yourself."

_____

Make It Yours

- What is your situation?

- What message do you need to Say it Now?

- What words or setting do you need to Say it Right?

- Is it time to be silent with someone or in some situation?

- Risks? If you Say it Now?

- Rewards?

CHAPTER 25

"You're Not The Boss Of Me." Taking On The Bullies

The Savannah Morning News (January 2, 2016) reported a story about a severely handicapped boy who was having lunch with his mother and another child at a local Subway restaurant. Another customer, Kevin Prisant, a running back coach at Benedictine Military School in Savannah, saw three teenage boys making fun of the handicapped boy – calling him names and making hand gestures. While Prisant was at the cash register, he told the boys to "…watch what they were saying and (I) suggested they apologize." The three teenagers apologized to the handicapped boy. The mother was appreciative. The other Subway customers gave Prisant a standing ovation. A customer who witnessed the incident called local media about the good deed, and it ended up as the headline story on the front page of the newspaper.

This situation had a happy ending. Many others don't. "Oh, it was just a joke." "I was just teasing you." "Lighten up…you take things too seriously." What one person thinks is a joke can be a devastating blow to someone with little or no self-esteem, confidence, or self-worth. It's not easy to spot the tough from the timid. When in doubt, be nice. Or, listen to your mother and don't say anything at all.

Bullies are a special situation because they don't try to hide their destructive behavior. Whether it's out in the open or via social media, texting, etc., most people know who their bullies are. Bullies get some sick pleasure out of being out there.

> What one person thinks is a joke can be a devastating blow to someone with little or no self-esteem, confidence, or self-worth.

They are also a special situation, because they are good at inflicting harm on others, whether it's physical, psychological, verbal, or digital. There are real risks when you Say it Now! to a bully. Like getting the ..it beat out of you. Even if you are taking up for someone else, speaking up can make the bully redirect his wrath at you.

In these situations, it's best to Say it Now! to someone else who is in a position of authority or has been trained in handling these situations, like law enforcement, a school counselor, psychologist, or in the workplace, Human Resources. Bullies can be just cowardly blowhards, or real life angry, mean people who don't care who they strike out at.

If your friend, family member, or co-worker is being bullied, be a friend, encourage them to get help, and be supportive in any way that you can. Encourage them to seek help from the police (if it's a case of stalking or harassment), a counselor, or a mental health professional. In the workplace, it's called harassment and it's illegal. Notify a manager or Human Resources. Say it Now! and say it often if someone is in harm's way. Don't be a hero. You can easily miscalculate the risk or the determination of the bully or the lengths they will go to.

If you are the one being bullied, say so early on. Don't try to hide or ignore it or think you can handle it alone. Bullies are like snipers. They like to hide and take their shots around corners and behind the bushes. Bring them out in the open early by calling them out (if you think you can and always with support) or with the help of someone in authority. Suffering in quiet desperation or fear can take a greater toll on you. Someone cares. Someone will help. Reach out and Say it Now! and Say it Early!

> Someone cares.
> Someone will help.

Make It Yours

- What is your situation?

- What message do you need to Say it Now?

- What words or setting do you need to Say it Right?

- Risks? If you Say it Now?

- Rewards?

CHAPTER 26

SAY IT RIGHT!
To Yourself

In previous chapters, I've discussed how to handle tough or tender conversations involving other people – family, friends, co-workers, the boss, customers, or an annoying stranger on the street. These interactions can be challenging for a lot of reasons, since you're dealing with another person who has a free will and can react and respond in a number of ways.

You can Say it Now! and Say it Right! or Say it Later. Separating yourself from people or a situation is also an option. We leave bosses and co-workers behind when we leave the office (or click "Leave the Meeting" working remotely). You can find a private spot at home away from family members or curl up alone on the couch with a bowl of popcorn, Netflix, and the cat. We don't have to answer the phone or texts or emails, leaving the stress of difficult conversations or making decisions involving other people for another day.

There are situations, however, where we can't seem to get away from problems, negative feedback, criticism, and harsh judgments. These conversations don't stop when we change locations or find a quiet spot alone. Though we are good at applying the principles of Say it Now! Say it Right! in interpersonal situations, we aren't as successful with this persistent foe. I'm talking about the conversations we have with ourselves. We can be our harshest critics. Quick to judge – and it's usually a negative verdict. They may sound something like this:

"You wasted last night binge-watching Outlander for the third time??? No wonder you're not getting your work done. You'll never get that raise."

"How could you eat the whole bag of cookies? You're never going to lose weight! You have no self-control!"

"He broke your date for the third time at the last minute? And you're texting him to say it's OK? Don't you have any self-respect? You're such a loser."

"I'm just not smart enough (or have the right education, or the right breaks, or had the right parents, or have enough money) to be successful. Better to accept my present job (partner, home, car, situation) than to hope for something better and be disappointed."

(insert your own script.)

The good news is we can change the tone of our inner conversations and learn to treat ourselves like the unique and amazing individuals that we are by using the three principles of Say it Now! Say it Right!

- Say it Now! When you find yourself criticizing or judging yourself, don't entertain those negative thoughts, mulling them over and over. Stop and acknowledge that they are just thoughts and you have the power to change them. You have the choice to beat yourself up or be kind to yourself as you would to your best friend.

How we think about a situation or decision can be far from reality, especially if we get lost in "what ifs" or conjure up consequences or other people's reactions that haven't happened yet. Say to yourself, "I messed up." Allow yourself to be human and make mistakes like everyone else. Be kind, forgive yourself, and focus on finding a positive solution. It is said that if you aren't making mistakes you're not trying. Consider it a learning experience, make a change if needed, and move forward.

- Say it Right! It is said that words can kill, and that goes for the ones we say to ourselves. "You're worthless." "That was a dumb thing to say." "You can't do anything right!" How quick we are to label ourselves. Maybe we are repeating things that were told to us as children, or by a boss, spouse, or teacher. Those words from our past come up automatically when we've failed at something, said the wrong thing, or didn't meet our own standards and expectations. The good thing is now, we can write our own script using words of encouragement, care, and forgiveness.

> Allow yourself to be human and make mistakes like everyone else.

- **The Right Motive.** There are hundreds of books written about learning to love and value yourself. Self-talk should always be uplifting, affirming, kind, and loving. Treat yourself well, be kind and generous. The words you say to yourself should be positive to build confidence and help you become the best version of yourself.

One way to quiet your inner critic is to set expectations, goals, and dreams for yourself. I once met a young man who was working as a bartender at a popular restaurant on Hilton Head Island. It was a slow night in the off-season, and we got to talking. In response to my question, "How did you come to work as a bartender?" he told me he was actually a lawyer. In fact, he graduated from one of the best Ivy League law schools in the country. He came from a family of lawyers. He was the only son, and his parents expected him to become a lawyer to carry on the tradition. He fulfilled their dream but found early on that he hated being a lawyer. After a few difficult, stressful years in a profession he didn't choose, he quit the family firm. He moved to Hilton Head, and with his experience tending bar in graduate school, he easily found a job. He was happy living his stress-free life doing work he was good at and enjoyed. The customers loved him and he had made lots of friends on the island. He had his days free for the beach, sailing or just hanging out with friends. He made great money as a bartender, more than enough to support his lifestyle. Most of all, it was the life he chose for himself.

> How much of the fear, doubt, and regret come from other people's expectations?

Was he going to do this long-term? He didn't know, but for now, he was at peace with himself. His family? Well, his parents weren't as pleased, but he had learned to be comfortable with their opinions and disappointment. He knew he had made the right decision for himself.

Listen to your inner critic. So much of the chatter is about past failures or decisions made and regretted, opportunities (money, people, relationships) lost or never acted on. How much of the fear and doubt and regret come from other people's expectations? In my family, the girls were expected to graduate from high school, get an office job, get married, and then have children. I had plans to be a famous journalist and writer, traveling the world, having amazing experiences with creative, artistic people. After a year and a half, my college education was ended by a family situation. Instead of finding a way to continue on my own, I gave up my dreams, left the University, and after a short time, got married and started a family. It has taken me a long time to silence my inner critic's voice over that decision. I've also learned just how brave and resilient I am, and over the years found my path and lived my dreams.

Social media and the constant barrage of advertising remind us every day of how we are lacking and have to do something to look better, feel better, be smarter, get richer. The message is you're falling short and need to up your game to be accepted, included, and loved. We often set higher standards for ourselves than others, and then are disappointed and critical when we fall short.

In 2020, I wrote a chapter for the Amazon best-selling book, *1 Habit: For a Thriving Home Office* (Ranked #1 Amazon New Releases, Amazon Best Seller - 1 Habit™ - The Book Series - 1 Habit™ can change your life forever!), about being your own "dream boss" when you work from home. I cited a LinkedIn survey that showed 75% of U.S. employees who left their jobs voluntarily made their exit because of a bad manager, not the job.

With so many working from home due to the Covid-19 pandemic, we've become our own boss, managing our time and workload. This was a welcome change for those who had to suffer under a toxic manager or difficult work situations. Now that you're the boss, you get to be the "dream boss" you always wanted. You have the freedom to do your thing your own way while still getting the work done. Here are some tips to silence the inner critics and guilty feelings (still in your jammies at lunchtime?) and get to work!

- A dream boss has a clear vision, plan, and short- and long-term goals. Take some time each morning to think, plan, and set reasonable goals for the day. Then get moving.

- Are you still getting up at 6a.m., putting on your work "uniform" and logging in by 6:15? You've always wanted a flexible schedule with plenty of time for life. Finally, you've got a dream boss (you!) who agrees.

- The boss and co-workers have been replaced by the partner, kids, parents, and dog who now compete for your time and attention. Be decisive and assertive. Say it Now! Say it Right! to establish some boundaries during "office" hours. Enlist their help. A dream boss works best in a friendly, fun place where all are respected and valued.

- Be nice to yourself. It takes time to get out of the mindset of going to an office or job controlled by someone else. You're the dream boss, remember? You can binge watch Netflix in the afternoon. You can read a story to your five-year-old or take the dog for a walk. Put some life in your work. A dream boss wants you to be happy and successful.

> Put some life in your work. A dream boss wants you to be happy and successful.

Learning to stop the negative self-talk and be good to yourself may not be easy. Comparing yourself to others and then being disappointed that you aren't as successful or good-looking or witty or brilliant or talented as someone else is a losing proposition. The only role for you is you – all the others are taken. I had to learn to be comfortable with myself and love my quirky, creative mind that got distracted and excited by new ideas and opportunities – traits that weren't always valued by an employer.

Brian Tracy, world-renowned International Speaker, Sales and Motivation Trainer, author of over 80 books, and Success Coach, says 95% of your emotions are determined by the way you talk to yourself. (Positive Affirmation: I Like Myself! - YouTube) Positive self-talk can make a huge difference in your life and success. He encourages the use of positive affirmations, probably the most famous is "I like myself." I found this affirmation when I was beginning my consulting business. I have to say it was a bit awkward at first, standing in front of the mirror in the morning, staring myself in the eyes and saying "I like myself, I like myself, I like myself" three times. I didn't have a lot of confidence in my new venture, had no clients and no connections, but that simple mantra repeated every morning helped build my confidence and self-esteem. I went out to face the world knowing that even if no one else did, I liked myself and believed I would be successful.

Using positive affirmations of your own can help build your confidence, improve job performance, and result in better relationships. Get rid of the inner critic and replace it with a chorus of positive, raving fans. It's your choice.

Make It Yours

- What is your situation?

- What message do you need to Say it Now?

- What words or setting do you need to Say it Right?

- Risks? If you Say it Now?

- Rewards?

CHAPTER 27

SAY IT NOW!
And Say It Loud
– #NotMeToo

In her mesmerizing acceptance speech for the 2018 Cecile B. DeMille Award at the Golden Globe Awards, (Oprah Winfrey: Recipient Of The Cecil B. deMille Award 2018 | Golden Globes) Oprah Winfrey challenged women to find their voice and speak out. She said that a new day was on the horizon, and that day is Now. Those brave women who spoke out at that time brought down some of the most powerful figures in the movie industry and the media. They started the ball rolling. Today, thousands of women swell the ranks of the #metoo movement and give courage to others to speak up.

It's *always* been the time for women to Say it Now! in those critical moments when pressured, forced, or intimidated by the threat of job loss, fear of abandonment, isolation, or violence. Now is the time to say No! instead of saying yes or nothing at all. It takes courage to take a stand in the moment – or years afterwards – to find your voice to protect yourself or someone else.

After high school graduation, I landed an executive assistant position at an advertising agency on Michigan Avenue on Chicago's near-North Side. It was the era of the real Mad Men. Though I lived in Gary, Indiana, the experience, salary, and excitement of working in the "big city" was worth the hour train ride back and forth every day.

_____

Now is the time to say NO! instead of saying yes or nothing at all.

_____

I reported to three account executives. It was a busy office, and I loved the professional yet casual atmosphere and could fend off the occasional harmless flirtatious comments from account executive #1 and #2.

Executive #3 was a different story. Each man had his own office phone line that would light up a button on my phone when they needed assistance. I dreaded when #3's phone button lit up and I heard, "I'd like you to come in and take some dictation." His office was always dark, with the blinds drawn. He claimed the glare hurt his eyes. He said he was distracted by the noise in the hallway and insisted I close the door and pull my chair close to his so I could hear him. As he talked, he would subtly roll his chair toward me, so our knees would touch. When I drew back, he advanced. The dictation would invariably switch from ad copy to how lonely he was, and would I come up to his lake house over the weekend to talk about my future at the agency. I didn't accept his offers, but it was clear to me that raises and promotions might just depend on accepting his occasional gifts, lunch invitations, and, eventually, a weekend at his lake retreat.

Did I speak out, strong and fearless and let him know I was uncomfortable and his inappropriate behavior had to stop? Did I report him to the Office Manager? Did I say, "No way, not me?" Unfortunately, no. Did I feel sickened and trapped and degraded? Yes! Like thousands of women who are now standing up against previous sexual harassment, I kept silent for fear of losing my job. I did avoid him, restrict my time in his office, and kept casual conversation to a bare minimum. A few months later, I accepted a promotion, removing me from further contact with him and the harassment.

While the ranks of the #metoo movement are swelling, the best hope for the future – a future without the fear and intimidation and harassment that so many women have endured in silence – is to raise up a generation of girls and young women who find their voice and speak up. Tell that boss or co-worker they aren't afraid of them, learn to be clear about what they will and will not tolerate from boyfriends or bosses or relatives or strangers. To find their voice, speak their truth.

How do you find your voice? By taking a risk. By being so clear about your own values and boundaries that once crossed, you spring into action, raise up your hand, and yell STOP! with your voice, body language, and emotions.

In her online blog post, *"In case you missed it, we're complicit: Sexual Harassment in the Workplace,"* (www.FutureswithoutViolence.org), Lisa Kim makes the point that sexual harassment, in many cases, isn't a well-kept secret. There are few secrets in the workplace. Things done and said in confidence or behind closed doors have a way of making headlines on the office grapevine or in viral texts. Someone knew about the Harvey Weinsteins, Bill Cosbys, and Charlie Roses but chose not to make waves.

Throughout this book, I encourage people to take a risk, find their voice, and speak their own truth. Chapter 16, "Danger Zone: Watch Out for the Slippery Slope," discusses how innocent workplace interactions can quickly deteriorate into uncomfortable situations when one party misinterprets attention or concern to mean romantic or sexual interest. Now, no conversation, close proximity, wardrobe choice or friendly personality is ever a defense for or an invitation to cross the line, but part of the "no way me too" movement is awareness and taking control of your environment and situations to lessen the opportunity for harassment.

Fran Liebowitz, author, speaker, and humorist, talks about her many jobs as a young woman in New York in the Netflix series, "Pretend It's a City." She drove a taxi and cleaned houses because she didn't want to wait tables like her friends even though they were making more money, "because I didn't want to have to be nice to men to get tips or to sleep with the manager of my shift, which was a common requirement then for being a waitress in New York." (Fran Lebowitz's 'Pretend It's A City' Is The NYC Trip You Can't Take Right Now | Iowa Public Radio).

It's not easy to know what people or situations to avoid, but making an informed choice by finding out what is and is not tolerated within an organization, job, or profession is a first step. Climbing the ladder and cracking the glass ceiling may come with a bigger office and paycheck, but at a higher cost. We all have the choice not to put ourselves in situations where there is a reputation of harassment, intimidation, and abuse. Whether it's a personal or professional situation, there are warning signs if you keep your mind and eyes open. My daughter always tells me, "You are the prize," and not to settle for anyone or any situation where I'm not treated with respect. It's flattering to be wanted; it's far better to be valued.

It's time to stop confusing the boardroom for the bedroom. You may find your soul mate at the office, or on the assembly line, in the restaurant kitchen, or in the cubicle two rows over. Let's hear it for love! But in my 22 years in Human Resources, I never read a job description that listed, "Endure and/or tolerate unwanted sexual advances, comments, or personal contact," listed as a job responsibility. Sexual harassment, unwanted physical contact, intimidation, emotional, mental, or physical abuse are not options under "Other Duties As Assigned." To attract and retain top talent, organizations need to establish new rules for workplace behavior to make it safe and comfortable for everyone to Say it Now! and Say it Right! without fear of retaliation or retribution.

> It's time to stop confusing the Boardroom for the bedroom.

Here are some tips to Say it Now! Say it Right!

- If a conversation or comment makes you uncomfortable, make sure the offender is aware of it. They may not realize it was offensive to you, but regardless of what they think, you need to set a boundary. You can say, "This conversation makes me uncomfortable," and then leave. Separate yourself from the person or group. No judgments needed.

- If an immediate response isn't possible, find a time and safe place to speak your truth. You can't tell someone else to live by your rules or adopt your standards, but you can make it clear how you feel and how you expect to be treated.

- No means No! Be assertive – words, voice tone, and body language. The first time. Steady eye contact. Stand up tall.

Calm, controlled, voice tone. Take the lead and speak your truth by letting the person know:

- o What they are doing to offend.

- o How that makes you feel.

- o What kind of behavior you expect.

- Not everyone will change their ways. Repeat offenders call for backup. In a work situation, go to Human Resources. Employment law is clear on what harassment is and is not. A pastor or community organization that deals with harassment or abuse is another option. If the person is threatening, physically abusive, or you feel you or your family are in an unsafe situation, call 911.

- Choose your environment. Don't allow yourself to be at the mercy of another person or group, or put yourself in a situation or location where you can't control your movements or exit.

- Know your limits. It's easy to get caught up in the moment, the occasion, or too many margaritas with the gang at the neighborhood bar after work. Buddy up with a trusted friend who will help when you ignore your personal boundaries or who can steer you away from a compromising or dangerous situation.

No woman should ever be a victim of sexual harassment. As women, we need to be aware of how powerful we are and how we are responsible for our actions. We may not be able to control every situation, but I believe we are 100% responsible for honest, timely, and direct communication on what will and will not be tolerated from a boss, lover, boyfriend, husband, partner, co-worker, or stranger on the street.

Learn to Say it Now! and Say it Right! My hope is with the next generation, including my daughter and granddaughters, and their realization of how empowered and strong they are to direct their lives, live their values, and insist on their boundaries, so they will never have a reason to say, #metoo.

Make It Yours

- What is your situation?

- What message do you need to Say it Now?

- What words or setting do you need to Say it Right?

- Risks? If you Say it Now?

- Rewards?

CHAPTER 28

"Does This (Dress, Pair Of Pants, Etc.) Make My Butt Look Big?"

Everyone has their "oops!" moments. How do you recover from a moment where you Said it Wrong!??

What husband, wife, boyfriend, girlfriend, or partner hasn't heard this loaded question? There is no good answer to that question except "No, of course not." The person's butt may look as big as the rear end of a Buick in those spandex pants, but you're not going to tell them. No, not you. No bully in the world is as dangerous as a spouse (partner, friend) who has been told that her butt looks too big.

There are other loaded questions that need not be honestly answered, like "Does my new haircut make me look younger (older, sexier, cuter, etc.)?" or "Why do you hate my mother (father, sister, friends, etc.) so much?", or "Did I say or do anything stupid when I got so drunk last night?" (Yeah, they did...do you want to tell them?) Tread lightly, especially if it's a spouse, parent, or boss.

One way to avoid the uncomfortable and unanswerable question is to be proactive in your comments to those you love and those who love you. Here are some things to say to create, build, keep, or salvage a relationship, friendship, working relationship after an "oops" comment. The time is always right to Say it Now!

> The three magic words, "I'm sorry I..." are a good starting point to open a conversation and clarify the situation.

- **I'm sorry.** This can mean you're sorry for what you did or said. Or just a general "I'm a sorry SOB for what I did or said." You can embellish those two powerful words with things like:...I said what I did ...I hurt your feelings...I forgot to...I'm an insensitive jerk. Just like giving appreciation or praise, (we'll get to that in a minute) it's a good idea to be specific. Now if you think you've done X, and the other person is angry because you did Y, you've got another problem. The three magic words, "I'm sorry I..." are a good starting point to open a conversation and clarify the situation.

- **I was wrong.** This is a little different than "I'm sorry." If you're the kind of person who always thinks she is right, and will argue to the death to prove it, "I was wrong" is music to the other person's ears. Admitting you were wrong diffuses anger. It shows you take the blame and responsibility for an outcome or decision. "I was wrong" shows you're vulnerable.

- **I care about you – when you really do.** I am the kind of person who likes to hear "I love you." Some people insist that if you say it often (more than once a year) that it won't mean much anymore. I disagree. The important thing to note is what is important to your spouse, girlfriend, boyfriend, child, parent, etc. This phrase is not so much about you.

- **I appreciate it.** What you're really saying is, "I appreciate you." Everyone likes to be appreciated. You may not love the other person, but you can appreciate them for who they are and what they do.

- **I believe in you.** One of the Dale Carnegie 30 principles is "Give a person a good reputation to live up to." In other words, let someone know that you have faith in them to deliver. You know they can do it. You have confidence in their abilities and you know they won't let you down. Set the expectation that you know that person will be successful, and most will rise to the occasion, not wanting to let you down. You may doubt yourself (often) but when someone lets you know they have confidence in your abilities, it's a great gift.

When someone asks a question and you already know what answer they are looking for (no, dear, you look fantastic in those new jogging shorts!), you may be doomed before you say a word. A look, raised eyebrows, or even just too long a pause before an answer can give your true feelings away. In those cases, it's better to use one of the introductory phrases and Say it Now! Before he/she goes out in public or thinks he can handle binge drinking with the crowd, or repeats "Um" and "you know" every other word in a presentation that makes the audience want to throw things…at them.

Make It Yours

- What is your situation?

- What message do you need to Say it Now?

- What words or setting do you need to Say it Right?

- Risks? If you Say it Now?

- Rewards?

CHAPTER 29

SAY IT NOW! SAY IT RIGHT!– And Let It Go...Prepare For Unpredictable Outcomes

Just because you Say it Now! and Say it Right! doesn't mean that everyone will applaud your honesty and courage. There are many possible outcomes. You have to be prepared for them all.

As a member of Toastmasters, I qualified to compete in the State of Georgia Annual District Toastmasters Speech Evaluation

Contest at the 2011 Fall Conference in Atlanta, Georgia. In this competition, a designated speaker gives a five- to seven-minute target speech, and Toastmasters from Divisions from all over the State compete for the best two- to three-minute evaluation of that speech. One year, I competed and won in every preliminary contest and then in the final speech evaluation contest in Atlanta for the State of Georgia. I was shocked when they called my name as the first-place winner, since I hadn't won anything before, let alone competed in a state-wide competition.

The following year, I repeated my climb through the ranks of preliminary competitions, winning at each level, and ended up in the finals in Atlanta again. The target speech for all the contestants in the evaluation competition was pretty technical, with a lot of computer and internet jargon in it. I was struggling to understand the target speech and could see that others in the audience were as well. In fact, I could see that after a few minutes, some in the audience had drifted off and didn't seem to be listening anymore.

A good evaluation is honest, tactful, with the intention of building up and giving helpful, positive feedback. I was also in a competition, so the safe thing would have been to soften or ignore the fact that the content was a little too technical and focus instead on the positive aspects. The best feedback, I felt, is honest and makes the biggest impact for the individual. So, I decided to take a risk and Say it Now! in my evaluation, and also try to Say it Right!

I gave what I thought was a positive but honest speech evaluation. I applauded the speaker for his good points and delivery, but also included some suggestions to further define difficult, technical jargon, or give more stories or examples to help non-techies understand the more technical aspects of his speech. After my turn, I took my seat in the audience, and was able to hear some of the other evaluations. They were powerful and on target. They were overall positive, and no one else cautioned the speaker to explain the technical jargon to keep the audience engaged. After my evaluation, I saw a fellow Toastmaster from my Club give me the "thumbs up" and lots of positive feedback from the crowd. but when the awards were given out, I didn't win a thing. I took a risk and said what I felt was the honest, most helpful feedback I could, but I heard later that some of the judges didn't think I was being "nice." That I was being negative. I also heard from others in the audience that I was spot on with my evaluation, and they didn't understand much of what the speaker said.

So, I checked myself. Was this the time to Say it Now!? Absolutely! This was a competition, and I had the stage. Did I Say it Right? Right motive? Check! Proper delivery? Check! Honest feedback? Check! Did I target the person instead of comment on the message? No! All boxes were checked in the right columns.

> Just because you Say It Now! and Say It Right! doesn't mean that everyone will applaud your honesty and courage.

Saying it Now! and Saying it Right! doesn't mean what you say will always be applauded and you'll win the prize (or promotion, or praise). Be prepared for a variety of reactions. Saying it Now! and Saying it Right! isn't about always anticipating the outcome and playing towards pleasing everyone. In fact, Saying it Right! can put people on edge or upset the status quo. Even if you Say it Right! you may end up offending someone. You may be misunderstood no matter how clear and concise you try to be. Taking the risk by Saying it Now! and Saying it Right! can end up with a variety of outcomes. Here are the most common:

They love you. The best reaction is one where people are overwhelmed with gratitude for your speaking out, telling the truth, saving them from themselves, helping them become aware of a shortcoming and helping them overcome it. In this case, "I love you" can mean I love that you were honest with me, or I love that you care enough about me to speak up for my own good.

Now, declaring your love for a co-worker because they reminded you that your late arrivals at meetings is becoming a problem for them, or to the barista at the coffee shop for remembering your special order would be out of line. But showing appreciation to a spouse, partner, or special someone who lovingly takes a risk to deal with a difficult situation can strengthen relationships. Speaking your truth out of love can be a risky yet powerful way to say "I love you!" Wow, that's the best message, especially if the feeling is mutual, and you acted out of real, genuine love for the other person. Bask in it. Revel in it. Enjoy it. This is the best possible personal positive outcome from deciding to Say it Now! and Say it Right!

Some people find it difficult to say that simple phrase, "I love you" and yet it's the one that most people long to hear. Don't hold back. Tell that special someone you love them. Don't let them walk away, leave for a trip, or even just leave the house for work in the morning without saying "I love you" to your children, your parents, your friends.

They hate you. This reaction can be both positive and negative. On the surface, saying "I hate you" doesn't seem positive in any way. But it may be just the reaction you were going for. Hate is a powerful emotion. A strong reaction. If you're going to Say it Now! to someone who is destroying his life with alcohol or drugs, or has a habit of texting and driving, or is headed for a disastrous and dangerous relationship, or is doing something that can get them killed or arrested, they may react with "I hate you!" for calling them out, bringing things out in the open. Interventions are meant to be confrontational and metaphorically "slap someone upside the head" with reality.

It's difficult to Say it Now! to someone you love and want to help and have them react with "I hate you!" Sometimes you have to risk losing a relationship with someone you love in order to bring them to their senses.

What they may hate is not you, but the truth of what you have to say. In this case, the way to Say it Right! is to be honest, specific, and forceful. Don't try to soften the blow. You may be saving someone's life. Strong words provoke strong reactions. Don't be surprised but keep your resolve. Greater things may come from your courage to Say it Right! and Say it Now!

They ignore you. Love and hate are strong emotions, but at least you know you made an impression and you got a reaction. Being ignored can be frustrating. Aggravating. Insulting. You gathered up all your courage, practiced your script, and took time to be sure you were going to Say it Right! And nothing. Even though you don't get the reaction you wanted, be sure that the person is thinking about what you said. You may not get the reaction you want right away. You may have to deal with someone ignoring you for a while. If this person is someone you interact with on a regular basis, be prepared for an uncomfortable, awkward relationship. You may find another time to Say it Now! again when the person is more receptive.

They disinvite you. I was invited to a neighbor's house for an informal get together one evening. Most of the other guests had pets, including our hosts. They spent time together walking their dogs around the neighborhood, and the conversation that evening was mostly about their dogs, and what they did, what they ate, where they walked, etc. Since I didn't have a dog, or any pet at the time, I didn't have much to say. One person came up to me and started talking about some trick her dog learned, and I guess I looked bored, and she asked me if I liked dogs. I said I did but wasn't much of a dog person. She looked surprised, and probably thought there was something wrong with me. Well, I haven't been invited back with the "dog people" again. I'm not a dog person, and I don't feel comfortable pretending to be something that I'm not, so I decided to Say it Now! in that instance and it cost me inclusion in the neighborhood social dog circle. Such is life.

They listen to you. They may just shock you and listen to what you say and take it to heart. Eureka! It worked! It's a good feeling to know that someone values what you say and makes a change for the better. But be careful. They may change their behavior, ways, beliefs, or relationships based on what you had to Say it Now! Provoking a change in someone else, even if it is positive, is a huge responsibility.

Say you tell your girlfriend that her boyfriend is cheating on her, and she should dump him fast...and she does. While you think it's the right thing to do, your suggestion isn't the only solution to the problem. She could talk to him to see what the issues are. His cheating could be a one-time lapse. People make mistakes. Wayward boyfriends (or girlfriends) aren't all low life, two-timing jerks who think of no one but themselves. Giving advice or Saying it Now! can be the turning point in someone else's life. Be careful what you say. They just might listen to you. Be there for the aftermath. Suddenly alone, your friend may turn to you to fill the lonely hours with long conversations or hanging out while he/she rehashes the lost relationship.

They take it to heart. They're not mad at what you said. They just get quiet, say "Hmmm," and walk away. They may say something like, "that's interesting." No positive or negative. You may think you haven't made an impression, but these people just need some time to think it over, or "noodle it." If you've said what you needed to say and Said it Right!, say no more. Saying it over again, or every time you see the person until you get a reaction can be the wrong move. Let them think. Let them process your suggestion or warning or idea for as long as it takes. You may never know what they think. What they do is another story. If you constantly harass them, pressing for some type of reaction, you may eventually make them angry, which is not what you want. Let things go. You've taken action. Leave the results to the other person.

You don't win the prize. I already told the story of how giving what I thought was the best, most honest speech evaluation cost me a repeat of a first-place finish in the Regional Toastmasters Evaluation Contest. There are always choices to make when you decide to Say it Now! and Say it Right! Winning a prize is nice. It feels good. But winning a prize at the cost of ignoring an opportunity to Say it Now! and Say it Right! can cause inner turmoil, disappointment, and regret.

What you have to say could be something important about yourself. You're not prepared for the presentation. You're not the right person for the job. That great idea that everyone is so excited about wasn't your idea – someone else should get the glory. The prize that you won is really the work of the entire team. What you have to say can actually prevent you from winning the prize. Say it Now! and Say it Right! To do otherwise would be dishonest. The greater disappointment would be for others when they find out you weren't truthful. It's better to be proactively honest instead of being revealed as a fraud. Winning the prize is never worth sacrificing your honesty and integrity.

> Winning the prize is never worth sacrificing your honesty and integrity.

You save the day (world, business). We all love stories of heroes. The person who saves someone from a burning building, gives CPR when all hope is lost and gets the heart beating again, or stops a crime from being committed.

Motivational, charismatic leaders step in at the critical moment and stir the crowd with words so powerful they are empowered to defeat the greatest foes, work long, hard hours to save the company, the harvest, the neighborhood, the world. Who can predict that your words, spoken to one person, a group or hundreds at a time – spoken with passion and honesty – can change the course of the day, the year, or history itself? Your words of encouragement to a struggling student can be just what they need to press on, finish high school or college, embark on a promising career, and start a business or non-profit to serve humanity. Your words of confidence and compassion could be the turning point for someone who is in despair, considering ending what they feel is a meaningless, painful life. You can save a situation, a person, a life, or the world if you have the courage to Say it Now! and Say it Right!

Make It Yours

- What is your situation?

- What message do you need to Say it Now?

- What words or setting do you need to Say it Right?

- Risks? If you Say it Now?

- Rewards?

SECTION IV

Wrapping It Up

CHAPTER 30

Where Do We Go From Here?

If you've gotten this far, you're probably saying to yourself – this makes so much sense! You've also probably thought of lots of situations where you could have said something but didn't for a variety of reasons. You probably have a list of situations where you need to learn to Say it Now! and Say it Right!

You can make an incredible difference if you can learn this simple act, to recognize opportunities to make an honest, timely statement in the right way for the right reasons. Once you become aware of the importance and

> The big bonus is the reduced stress you will experience when you say what is in your heart for the right reasons.

impact these statements can make in a situation or to a person, it's an easy decision.

The big bonus is the reduced stress you will experience when you say what is in your heart for the right reasons. Just think of how much stress you experience trying to decide whether or not to speak up in a meeting. Should I speak up? Will they think the idea is stupid? Will no one react at all? Everyone will be looking at me. When you realize that not speaking up is a poor decision for so many reasons (one of which you won't get the recognition for a great idea), the stress falls away.

Sometimes the person we talk to the most and see all the time doesn't listen at all. It's the one who we see in the mirror every morning and night. I know I'm not the only one who has heart-to-heart talks with myself. Even given a lecture or two.

There are people and situations in our own lives that we are aware of, and we may be Saying it Now! over and over again without any result. That one glass of wine to relax after a hard day at work is now becoming half a bottle – every night. Your obsession with online shopping is getting out of hand, but no one is aware but you. What began as a harmless flirtation at the office has crossed the line, but the attention you're getting is too seductive to let it go. Your life is boring and your partner (spouse) is too busy with work, or community obligations, or sports or (fill in the blank), and you feel alone and unloved. The last child is out of the house, and you're faced with the truth that you desperately want to pack your bags and catch the next flight out of town, too.

These are tough situations to face. You may have been Saying it Now! to yourself – I need to stop drinking so much or get some help from a counselor; I'm out of control with the online spending; the flirtation is going too far. If self-talk doesn't work, it's time to Say it Now! to a counselor, pastor, friend, or hot-line (AA, your company's EAP) so someone else can Say it Now! and Say it Right!

to you. Give yourself the care and love you give someone else who needs to have someone Say it Now!

In my role as an HR Director, I had lots of opportunities where I could or should say something. I understand the pressure employees face when speaking up. There are risks and real fears. But the freedom you gain from learning how to say what you need to in the right way to achieve a positive result is life changing. I hesitated before writing that last sentence, because I don't want to sound cheesy and like some kind of motivational huckster. It's real. It's not a big thing, but it is a freeing feeling. If you get some tips and techniques to put the Say it Now! Say it Right! method into practice, the book was worth it.

Make It Your Own — Find Your Voice

CHAPTER 31

Make It Your Own

If you bought this as a "real" book, you probably highlighted certain passages, or turned down a few page corners to mark sections you want to go back to. If you're reading this on a Kindle or other device, you may have used the electronic underline, highlighter, or page marker to do the same. I like to mark book sections that I can easily spot so I can find the "nuggets" that are most meaningful.

I've given you a lot of things to think about. The art of Say it Now! Say it Right! is not frequency. There is no urgency to find situations every day, or every hour. No, this technique is best used sparingly, lest you come across as everyone's critic or judge. Or someone who just wants to hog the spotlight.

You can refer back to this section to remind yourself of just how you can use Say it Now! and Say it Right! in your own life to achieve your own goals.

- Is it less stress?

- Truly helping people who may be unaware of obstacles easily overcome in their personal or professional lives?

- Intervening in a situation to prevent harm or abuse?

- Overcoming your own awkwardness and finally letting those close to you know how much you love and care about them?

- Or taking the time to point out the positive things people are doing by Saying it Now! and Saying it Right?

Before you close the book, take a moment to go back through and make some notes in the next section to really make this your own.

"Proclaim the Truth and do not be silent through fear." Catherine of Sienna

CHAPTER 32

What Is Your "IT!?"

What is your IT! that so desperately needs to be said Now!? Everyone has their own personal situations, events, and opportunities to Say it Now! and Say it Right! If you've gotten this far, you may have recalled your own Julie story, or broccoli in the teeth moment, or thought of a situation or conversation you've been avoiding at work or at home. Or a situation in the community that you feel passionate about. Or a great idea that you've been reluctant to share or act upon. Knowing your "IT!" is the first step. The next is recognizing your opportunity to Say it Now! and the way to Say it Right!

What is this IT! that you just have to say? IT could be a lot of things, such as:

- IT could be an opposing viewpoint.

- IT could be Stop! Get Out of the Way, as in get out of the way of that car that's speeding toward you before you get run over!

- IT could be a great idea that you've come up with.

- IT could be an innovative way to solve a problem.

- IT could be an annoying personal habit or trait that someone has but is unaware of (picking teeth, licking lips, saying "like" or "awesome" every other word, saying "OK" or "UM" or "AH" over and over when speaking).

- IT could be "No!"

- IT could be "Yes" despite opposing viewpoints.

- IT could be holding staff responsible for performance.

- IT could be giving an authentic, honest performance review to an underperforming manager for the first time.

- IT could be standing up in a group of senior managers to oppose a course of action you know, from first-hand experience, could be a disaster.

- IT could be "I Love You," even if the other person doesn't feel the same way.

- IT could be "I Love You," when you've withheld saying it for so many reasons to a spouse, loved one, child, or friend.

- IT could be "I Love You" to the person staring back at you in the mirror – yourself.

- IT could be STOP! Without an apology or defense. You're worth it.

IT could be a lot of things. The IT varies, but the Say it Now! means don't wait. Take the moment. Don't let it pass. Don't put it off when NOW is the best time and will have the best effect. IT means Say it Now! or you may never have another chance to say it again with the same force or meaning.

If I had waited to say something to my friend Julie's father, she may have endured a dire punishment. In some situations, there is no other chance to intervene and prevent something from happening or make it happen than that moment. If you don't Say it Now! you may never have the chance to say IT in quite the same way again. Or at all.

> If you don't Say It Now! you may never have the chance to say IT in quite the same way again. Or at all.

Practice:

What's Your IT?

Think back to times in your life where you had an IT situation but didn't Say it Now! What were those situations? What could you have said? If you had taken the risk to Say it Now! what would have been the outcome?

- List three situations where you had the opportunity to Say it Now! but didn't take the chance.

- What were the consequences?

- What could have happened if you had spoken up at that time?

- How could your life, or the life of someone else, been changed or affected if you had spoken up?

Now, think of those situations where you did Say it Now! but missed the mark on Say it Right! What happened? Bad timing? Wrong motive? Poor phrasing? Too public? Too impulsive? Have you had an opportunity for a "do over?" How did the second chance work out? Just because you said it wrong the first time doesn't mean you can't try again.

Use some of the phrases in the previous chapters and try again. This is the perfect place to think back and plan your second chances. Apologize for the method, not the message. If you have trouble saying the words "I'm sorry," you can always say you regret the situation, or the way you came across, or the bad timing, or whatever your blunder. Then, declare your honest, heartfelt motive and then restate your Say it Now!

> Just because you said it wrong the first time doesn't mean you can't try again.

For example,

"Jerry, I regret that I came across judgmental and abrupt the last time we talked about your new project idea. I felt it was important to share my reservations in the meeting so we could get input from the rest of the team, but I know now that it would have been better to share my feelings with you first before the meeting. I didn't mean to put you on the spot." (Give time to hear Jerry out and have an open conversation, then continue.) "I still feel strongly that the project should be restructured with a lower budget. Can you bring me some ways to make that happen before the next meeting? Thanks."

Say it Now! Say it Right! applies to apologies and regrets and seeking second chances. If what you have to say is truly important (critical) for the other person to hear the first time, you can't just let it go because of a poor delivery. On the other hand, if it wasn't that critical, then check your motives for saying it at all.

There is an expression, "Hindsight is 20-20." Things are always clearer when you can look back at a situation rather than while you're experiencing it. Things move fast, and it's difficult to recognize those moments when you need to speak up.

CHAPTER 33

My Personal Strategy To SAY IT NOW! AND SAY IT RIGHT!

What are the situations where I haven't said what I needed to say in a timely manner?

1.
2.
3.

What is holding me back from Saying it Now! and Saying it Right!?

1.

2.

3.

If I take the risk to Say it Now! and Say it Right!, what are the positive outcomes I can expect? How will my life be better? Happier? More fulfilling?

1.

2.

3.

What are some of the ways that I've Said it Wrong? Wrong words, places, settings?

1.

2.

3.

What situations exist now where I can Say it Now! and Say it Right?

1. In the workplace?

2. In my personal life?

3. In my community?

Endorsements

"This brilliant book is a communication roadmap to strategically guide you from where you are to where you want to be. Do you want healthy, supportive relationships wherein everyone feels safe enough to express their needs in a clear, concise, and respectful way? Then buy this book. In fact, buy several copies so you can share it with people you love and/or work with. Watch everyone's life transform for the better."

Linda Larsen, author, *12 Secrets to High Self-Esteem*

"With honesty, humor and solid advice, Mary Nestor shows us how to find our voice, summon our courage, and have the often uncomfortable or difficult conversations we have been avoiding. *SAY IT NOW! SAY IT RIGHT!* is a must-have guide for personal use and is equally indispensable in the workplace."

Chaz Pitts-Kyser, author, *Careeranista: The Woman's Guide to Success After College*

"*SAY IT NOW! SAY IT RIGHT!* is a no-nonsense, straightforward book about a very important topic in business and interpersonal relationships today. Mary Nestor provides solid content and presents it through engaging stories readers can relate to with practical tips to use immediately. This book should be required reading for anyone in business and government leadership positions."

Dr. Tony Alessandra, author, *Communicating at Work and The Platinum Rule*

"This fast-moving, entertaining book gives you the exact words to say to feel confident and in control of any conversation."
Brian Tracy, author, *Speak to Win*

"Mary Nestor's book *SAY IT NOW! SAY IT RIGHT!* reminds us of the urgency and importance of our communication skills. We often realize this; however, rarely has anyone given us the words and guide for the many situations we find ourselves in. The situations themselves may be unplanned; however, with Mary's book you will not be unprepared."
Patricia Fripp, CSP, CPAE; Past President, National Speaker's Association

"It's time someone spoke out on speaking up! Read this book and turn up your volume for success now!"
Jeffrey Hayzlett, Primetime TV & Podcast Host, Chairman C-Suite Network

"*SAY IT NOW! SAY IT RIGHT!* should be required reading for CEOs, leaders, managers…anyone who has ever hesitated to speak up in critical moments in business, relationships, and life. You will dramatically improve your influence, impact, and income when you learn to Say it Now! and Say it Right!"
David Newman, author, *Do It! Marketing*

About the Author

Mary J. Nestor is founder and director of MJN Consulting, an international leadership, communications, and organizational change company. She is an award-winning, highly sought-after international speaker, best-selling author, executive coach, trainer, and consultant. She works with individuals and organizations to get people talking...tackling the tough issues with open, honest, and respectful communication that gets them unstuck and growing again. She has the ability to get all levels of an organization working together through dynamic in-person or virtual keynotes, training seminars, consulting, and coaching.

Mary has over 25 years' experience as a Human Resources director in both corporate and non-profit sectors. She is a certified coach and trainer through the John Maxwell Group, holds the SHRM-SCP certification in Human Resources, and is a 25-year member of the National Speakers Association. She was certified in Total Quality Management/Statistical Process Control by the British Standards Institute (BSI) and has led ISO 9000 certification projects for both Monsanto Company and Garrett Aviation

(Augusta, GA). She is past president of the Savannah Toastmasters Club #700.

She began her writing career as a columnist for the Augusta (GA) Business Journal, and has written hundreds of feature stories, blogs, and articles for The Savannah Morning News and various clients and online business websites. *SAY IT NOW! SAY IT RIGHT!* is her second book, about which Jim Cathcart, Past President of the National Speakers Association and author of *Relationship Selling*, said, "*SAY IT NOW! SAY IT RIGHT!* may be the most valuable book you ever read." She is a contributor to two books in the #1 Best-Selling 1 Habit book series. Her next project is a soon-to-be released mystery/thriller novel.

Originally from the Midwest, Mary moved to Hilton Head Island, South Carolina, after 14 years living in a 160-year-old row house in Savannah Georgia's Historic District. She sings Alto II with the Savannah Symphony Orchestra and Chorus and the St. John the Baptist Cathedral/Basilica Choir. When she's not playing Pickleball or golf, she is part of a team of talented women fabricating home furnishings at a custom sewing house in Savannah. She also enjoys spending time with her two married children and five grandchildren.